FOOD AND THE RITES OF PASSAGE

First published in 2002 by Prospect Books, Allaleigh House, Blackawton, Totnes, Devon TQ9 7DL.

Based on papers from the Fourteenth Leeds Symposium on Food History, April 1999. This is the eleventh volume in the series 'Food and Society'.

© 2002 as a collection, Prospect Books (but © 2002 in individual articles rests with the individual authors).

The authors assert their right to be identified as the authors of their several pieces in accordance with the Copyright, Designs & Patents Act 1988.

No part of this publication may be reproduced, stored in a retrieval system, or transmitted in any form or by any means, electronic, mechanical, photocopying, or otherwise, without the prior permission of the copyright holder.

BRITISH LIBRARY CATALOGUING IN PUBLICATION DATA:
A catalogue entry for this book is available from the British Library.

ISBN 1 903018 17 X

Typeset by Tom Jaine.
Printed and bound by the Cromwell Press, Trowbridge, Wiltshire.

Contents

List of Illustrations	6
Notes on Contributors	7
Foreword *C. Anne Wilson*	8
Introduction *Laura Mason*	10
Chapter 1 Ritual Structure and the Dramaturgy of Food in the Context of the Late Twentieth-century Wedding *Tony Green*	15
Chapter 2 Bridecup and Cake: The Ceremonial Food and Drink of the Bridal Procession *Ivan Day*	33
Chapter 3 'She came from a groaning very cheerful …' Food in pregnancy, childbirth and christening ritual *Layinka Swinburne and Laura Mason*	62
Chapter 4 Arvals, Wakes and Month's Minds: Food for Funerals *Peter Brears*	87
Chapter 5 Food and Drink at Irish Weddings and Wakes *Regina Sexton*	115
Chapter 6 Recipes	143
Bibliography	155
Index	161

List of Illustrations

Figure 1. Detail from Joris Hoefnagel's 'A Wedding Fête at Bermondsey', *c.* 1569–1571. This painting is discussed in the chapter by Ivan Day, below. (Reproduction is by courtesy of the Marquess of Salisbury.)   2

Figure 2. Wrapping used by E.S. & A. Robinson, packaging manufacturers of Bristol showing the first cutting of a single (untiered) bride-cake, decorated with white icing.   18

Figure 3. An illustration, taken from the 1901 edition of Isabella Beeton's *Household Management*, depicting the arrangement and components of a buffet wedding tea.   24

Figure 4. A seventeenth-century woodcut showing the attendants on a bride sporting sprigs of rosemary tied to their arms.   34

Figure 5. Joris Hoefnagel, 'A Wedding Fête at Bermondsey', *c.* 1569–1571. (Reproduction by courtesy of the Marquess of Salisbury.)   42

Figure 6. Shew bread, from the Geneva Bible, 1650.   46

Figure 7. A marchpane, embellished with sprigs of rosemary decorated with gilded lozenges, ornamented with sugar-paste clove gillyflowers or carnations, as depicted in a still life by the Dutch painter Clara Peeters (*fl.* 1600–20), in *c.* 1615.   48

Figure 8. A jumble in the form of lovers' knot, as depicted in a still life by the Dutch painter Clara Peeters (*fl.* 1600–20), in *c.* 1615.   50

Figure 9. Figure for an 'extraordinary Pie, or a Bride Pie of several Compounds, being several distinct Pies on one Bottom', from Robert May's *The Accomplist Cook* (1660).   52

Figure 10. Tansy, an engraving from Culpeper.   64

Figure 11. Apostle spoons, a traditional gift from godparent to godchild. From William Hone, *The Every-day Book*, 1838.   80

Figure 12. A stone mould for funeral biscuits, once in the possession of Thomas Beckwith of York. (Drawing by Peter Brears.)   102

Figure 13. A sycamore mould for funeral biscuits, once belonging to Mrs Nelson of Burton-in-Lonsdale, now in York Castle Museum. (Drawing by Peter Brears.)   102

Figure 14. Printed paper wrappers for finger-shaped funeral biscuits, produced in Leeds around the years 1816–1825.   104

Figure 15. Wrapper for funeral biscuits, dating from approximately 1816–1825.   106

Figure 16. Wrapper for funeral biscuits, late nineteenth century.   106

Notes on Contributors

PETER BREARS is a regular contributor to the 'Food and Society' series. He is a museum and historic-house consultant as well as food historian, and has been involved in the restoration of the Tudor kitchens at Hampton Court.

IVAN DAY is a food historian with a special interest in re-creating the food of the past in period settings. His work has been exhibited at Fairfax House, York; the Bowes Museum; the Rothschild Collection, Waddeson Manor; the Museum of London; and the Paul Getty Research Institute. He is editor of *Eat, Drink and Be Merry: the British at table 1600–2000*.

TONY GREEN was born in Birmingham and lives in Leeds. he has worked in University College, London, the Memorial University of Newfoundland, the University of Leeds, and Bretton Hall College where he is senior lecturer in Theatre. He is an historian and anthropologist of performance.

LAURA MASON is a food historian. Her work includes *Traditional Foods of Britain* (with Catherine Brown), and *Sugar Plums and Sherbet*, a history of sugar confectionery in Britain since the Middle Ages. She lives in Yorkshire.

REGINA SEXTON is a food historian living in County Cork. Ireland. Her area of special interest is early medieval Ireland but she has published widely, at both an academic and popular level, outside this period. She is co-author of the EU survey, *Ireland's Traditional Foods* (1997) and author of *A Little History of Irish Food* (1998).

LAYINKA M. SWINBURNE has extended her interest in nutritional medicine to food history, exploring the overlapping fields of cookery and domestic medicine in the early modern period.

Foreword

The Leeds Symposium on Food History was founded in 1986 by four food historians at Leeds: Peter Brears, Lynette Hunter, Jennifer Stead and Anne Wilson. We were already in touch with one another, partly because we all at various times consulted the early cookery book collections at the Brotherton Library, University of Leeds, where I worked as an assistant librarian. We decided to hold a one-day annual conference in April, for which a food history theme would be chosen and speakers would discuss different aspects of that theme. The first four meetings (1986–89) were supported by the University's Department of Adult Education; and for subsequent meetings until 1997 we had secretarial support from the School of English. Now in today's less clement economic climate we are 'on our own', and the organization of the Symposium rests entirely with our committee of five and with a few volunteers, for whose help we are most grateful.

From the beginning we planned to publish our papers, believing that books on particular topics of food history would be of interest to a far wider readership than those people able to attend the Symposium meetings. The first volume, 'Banquetting Stuffe', was based solely on the talks given at the 1986 Symposium. But thereafter we included additional chapters to cover further unexplored facets of our subject, and some of these were contributed by historians other than the speakers at the Symposium.

The first six volumes were published by Edinburgh University Press; the following three by Sutton Publishing (two of them in association with the National Trust), 1994–98; the last two volumes have been issued by Prospect Books. All are in the Food and Society Series, and although nos. 1–7 are now out of print, copies can sometimes be obtained from the specialist firms selling second-hand cookery and food history books by mail order.

The titles, with the series numbers, are:-
1. *'Banquetting Stuffe': the Fare and Social Background of the Tudor and Stuart Banquet*, ed. C.A. Wilson (1986 Symposium), 1991.
2. *The Appetite and the Eye: Visual Aspects of Food and its Presentation within their Historic Context*, ed. C.A. Wilson (1987 Symposium), 1991.
3. *Traditional Food East and West of the Pennines*, ed. C.A. Wilson (1988 Symposium), 1991.

INTRODUCTION

4. *Waste Not, Want Not: Food Preservation in Britain from Early Times to the Present Day*, ed. C.A. Wilson (1989 Symposium), 1991.

5. *Liquid Nourishment: Potable Foods and Stimulating Drinks*, ed. C.A. Wilson (1990 Symposium), 1993.

6. *Food for the Community: Special Diets for Special Groups*, ed. C.A. Wilson (1991 Symposium), 1993.

7. *Luncheon, Nuncheon and Other Meals: Eating with the Victorians*, ed. C.A. Wilson (1992 Symposium), 1994.

8. *The Country House Kitchen, 1650-1900: Skills and Equipment for Food Provisioning*, ed. P. A. Sambrook and P. Brears (double volume for 1993 and 1994 Symposia), 1996.

9. *The Country House Kitchen Garden, 1600-1950: How Produce was Grown and How it was Used*, ed. C.A. Wilson (1995 Symposium), 1998.

10. *Feeding a City: York*, ed. Eileen White (1997 Symposium), 2000.

The volume for the 1996 Symposium, titled 'Chopping and Changing: Cutlery and its Usage', is not yet published.

C. Anne Wilson
Brotherton Library, University of Leeds

INTRODUCTION

Laura Mason

This book is based on papers presented at the fourteenth Leeds Symposium on Food History. The initial idea of covering food customs 'from cradle to grave' was narrowed to examine the three major rites of passage – christening, marriage and burial – in the British Isles. They are viewed principally within the dominant framework of Anglican Christianity, with an excursion into Irish Catholicism.

In any culture, food and drink are important elements of rituals surrounding major life events. In English, a celebration is now taken colloquially to mean a party or festivity, with plenty to eat and drink; but the primary meaning is the public performance of a solemn ceremony, especially a religious one. In Christianity, the link with food is implicit: the bread and wine of the Eucharist are at the core of the religion.

Even in early twentieth-century Britain, where food was largely undiscussed, there was a consensus about what was proper at festivities. Witness the efforts made in wartime, providing wedding 'cakes' of plaster 'icing' over a cardboard base when eggs, butter and dried fruit were unobtainable. The image was there, if not the reality. Although food and food-related customs are the primary considerations here, the significance of the events to which they are attached means that more than nourishment is involved in the discussions below. Food was also symbolic, and ritual included it with categories of non-edibles, such as spoons, cups, gloves and wedding rings. The 'logic', for want of a better word, behind all this has been little explored, at least by food historians. For a discussion of some religious and cultural background, see David Cressy's book *Birth, Marriage and Death: ritual religion and the lifecycle in Tudor and Stuart England*.

In the papers given here, Tony Green sets the scene by considering late twentieth-century wedding customs in an ethnographic framework. He looks at the dynamics of the ritual, types of meal, and relationships between colour in clothes and cakes. Ivan Day's chapter extends the history of wedding foods back into the early modern period, revealing customs quite unlike our own 'traditional' ones.

Proceeding from this, the next chapter is on birthing and christening children. Layinka Swinburne provides a glimpse into some of the informal

Introduction

customs surrounding pregnancy and birth. This is a notoriously difficult subject to research; little was recorded about pregnancy and childbearing, which was part of the undisclosed world of women. More public and formal food customs associated with christening are summarized by Laura Mason. The division between informal and formal in birth rituals varied. The junction occurred somewhere around the 'gossiping', the gathering which provided support to the woman in labour, but it is confounded by factors linked to status, fashion and gender. Although these two authors originally presented their papers separately, for clarity's sake they have been made into one chapter.

The role of food in funerals and mourning ritual is considered by Peter Brears, who shows some elaborate and status-bound customs relating to this aspect of the life-cycle, and illustrates how doles and other remembrances were used to keep the dead in the minds of the living. Finally, taking a view from within a different but related culture, Regina Sexton looks at food and drink associated with weddings and funerals in Ireland, emphasising how even people labouring against the most adverse and extreme poverty still celebrated marriages and wakes with lavish, even reckless, hospitality.

Time and space did not allow an examination of the practices of other sects or religions. Nor are the papers here intended to form a complete view of the subject; this is impossible in the limited space available. The divinatory and superstitious uses of food in customs such as forecasting the identity and disposition of a future spouse, and sin-eating on behalf of the departed, receive some attention. The use of food in lesser rituals awaits exploration. Birthdays, anniversaries, confirmations, exam success and comings-of-age are ignored in the work presented here. Food and drink in courtship ritual and the engagement party (or its precursor, the formal betrothal) are not examined, nor are the phenomena of stag nights and hen parties.

The cyclical nature of life – renewal and decay – presents a logistic problem within the linear framework of a book. The reader may question the logic of commencing with weddings, but there are good reasons for looking at this first. Romantic novelists would have us believe such an event is an end in itself; but it is also a beginning, the creation of a new unit, through which society has validated childbearing for hundreds of years. And, like all rituals, it is an opportunity to display wealth and status. In the past it was much more than a sanction of a sexual relationship for begetting legitimate heirs. Although the attitude of the Church has been ambivalent at times, it was often included among the sacraments. It was a means of property transfer, and method of cementing alliances between families, or even countries; hence the edifice of display and superstition which surrounds the process. Apart from adult baptism, it is the only one of the three major rites of passage where those going through it are conscious of what they are doing (at least, one hopes they are). In a modern context, it has become the most visible of the three ceremonies.

It is also the one ritual without a model in the paradigm of the life of the Holy Family. The Christian year provides a prototype of the human life-cycle, repeated annually: a birth (Christmas) and a death (Easter), and a churching (Candlemas, or the Purification of the Virgin Mary). There is also, not directly linked to the life of the holy family, a remembrance of the dead at All Souls (1 November) which had its own special foods and internal logic. Such holy days involved preparation in the form of fasting followed by feast days with symbolic foods, especially breads.

This ritual year must have served to keep the human life-cycle present in people's minds at all times, whilst perhaps providing some ideals for society generally. But there is no wedding in this annual round; no anniversary is assigned to the Wedding Feast at Cana or any other. Attitudes to other calendar events which celebrated fecundity or sexuality varied. Harvest Home has been subdued and incorporated into the liturgical year as the Harvest Festival. Carnival, a time of licence and excess, and May Day have both largely disappeared from British customs. It is true that the holy year involves the Annunciation; but that emphasizes and sets aside the Virgin Mary from humanity. It is not the same thing as a wedding, as pregnant, unwed women have always known. So, bearing in mind that it is an event both extraordinary in and integral to life-cycle ritual since the Middle Ages, the wedding is a fitting starting point.

At the level of eating, there is a good reason for relating the foods associated with the human life-cycle to the practices of the church. This is the fundamental importance of bread and wine in celebrations. Before the Reformation, both baptism and marriage were numbered among the sacraments, and burial was normally accompanied by a Mass; thus, the celebrants fasted beforehand and broke their fast with consecrated wafers and wine. 'Cakes and ale', or wine, are secular reflections of this; and one suspects that they were the common food and drink with which poorer people celebrated every festival and joyous event. This aspect of ritual is just one manifestation

Introduction

of the importance of Christianity in medieval and early modern lives. Keith Thomas observed in *Religion and The Decline of Magic*:

> Like the Mass, the other Christian sacraments all generated a corpus of parasitic beliefs, which attributed to each ceremony a material significance which the leaders of the Church had never claimed. By the eve of the Reformation most of these rituals had become crucial 'rites of passage', designed to ease an individual's transition from one social state to another, to emphasize his new status and secure divine blessing for it.

Ivan Day and Peter Brears show in their papers that early modern practice included the distribution of bread or cakes at weddings and funerals, and that they were thought to have mystical properties. Thomas did not discuss food, but made the following observation about the manner in which superstitions generally accumulated:

> It is hardly necessary to detail the allied superstitions which attached themselves to the ceremony of marriage. Most of them taught that the fate of the alliance could be adversely affected by the breach of a large number of ritual requirements relating to the time and place of the ceremony, the dress of the bride, and so forth. Typical was the notion that the wedding ring would constitute an effective recipe against unkindness and discord, so long as the bride continued to wear it. Such notions provide a further demonstration of how every sacrament of the church tended to generate its attendant sub-superstitions which endowed the spiritual formulae of the theologians with crude material efficacy.

This tendency was perhaps less apparent in the various rituals accompanying the burial of the dead, such as the convention that the corpse should face East or that the funeral should be accompanied by doles to the poor.

The overt link with religion has been broken, first by the religious turmoil of the sixteenth and seventeenth centuries, and then by industrialization and secularization of society. But the ideal of bread and wine as the archetypal symbolic meal is buried deep in the idea of ritual, and can be traced down several routes. In addition to their use at Mass, wafers and wine were the principal elements of the *voidee*, the final sweet element of a medieval meal. 'Spices', sugar-coated comfits, were incorporated into this by the early modern period; these, too, were a significant presence at births and weddings, although this is not obvious from modern British practice. The

INTRODUCTION

voidee later evolved into the dessert, which itself was an important element of grand celebratory meals.

The essays are primarily concerned with food, and their scope (with the exception of the first chapter) does not extend to sociological or anthropological analyses. What does emerge is a clear picture of customs adapting slowly to circumstances. Early modern religious reforms forced a change in numerous social customs; this is particularly apparent in relation to the bride-cake. Closer to the twentieth century, it is science which altered things. Developments in ingredients and cooking techniques changed the form of cakes themselves. Understanding of hygiene and nutrition led to changes in many customs surrounding childbirth and infant feeding, often (but not invariably) to the benefit of mother and child. Modern distaste for facing the material fact of death means the funeral biscuit has been forgotten, although most people still feel the need for a relaxed social gathering after the stress of a burial or cremation service.

Because of the fundamental importance of birth, marriage and death, rituals associated with them continue, as the wider expression of individual family circumstance. Formerly, the events considered here were once matters for entire communities, in which most members could expect to participate somehow, often receiving some edible token in the process. Except for the royal family and a few other national figures, the ceremonies are increasingly privatized. Change does not only relate directly to food. One of the most striking examples is the loss of the 'processional' aspect of ceremonies. It is true that bridal couples have ribbon-decked vintage cars, and corpses have gleaming black hearses. But where the rituals were formerly events whose participants could be viewed and followed as they walked or used horse transport to the church, cars and increasing distance (between relatives, home, church, cemetery) have turned them into relatively anonymous happenings, controlled, among other things, by access to transport. And no-one parades a bride-cake to be blessed in church any longer.

CHAPTER ONE

Ritual Structure and the Dramaturgy of Food in the Context of the Late Twentieth-century Wedding

Tony Green

To begin, why dramaturgy? Why not the less recondite and, in many ways, more useful term *imagery*? But first, 'imagery' tends aesthetically to imply that which is static: the iconography of a picture or the figurative language of a printed poem, rather than dynamic; and, whatever else, rituals are nothing if not dynamic. Paradoxically, while an appeal to the past and a respect for tradition are characteristic of them, their basic function is to organize the future. Second, especially in a century which has witnessed the widespread use of the still-camera (and now the camcorder) for the recording of actuality, the notion of 'imagery' carries with it, culturally, no necessary connotation of fiction.

Whereas 'dramaturgy' necessarily connotes fiction, an important point in an essay on the *rite de passage*. For ease of exemplification, I shall concentrate on the solemnization of matrimony in the practice of the Church of England in our own time; and this raises issues, both methodological and substantive, with which the notion of dramaturgy may help. First, the methodological issue. In an important article and subsequent book, *Wedding Cakes and Cultural History*,[1] addressed in part to the subject here, Dr Simon Charsley concerns himself with the phenomenology of cultural meaning. He is particularly interested in that long-standing anthropological conundrum: whether it is legitimate to attribute a given meaning to a given social action, when it cannot be shown that the social actor is aware of that meaning. This is not the place to debate the subject at length (an adroit summary has been made by Brenda Neale, again with precise reference to the immediate subject-matter[2]). Since the approach used here might be questioned by Dr Charsley, I ought briefly to outline my position.

Ritual Structure and the Dramaturgy of Food

I find no difficulty in accepting that human beings are fluent and inventive acquirers and users of sign-systems, whilst also being generally incompetent at explaining how and why they do it, or precisely what it is they are doing. An obvious example is language: native speakers regularly and (more or less) faultlessly produce original utterances in their communication with other native speakers, who instantaneously and (more or less) faultlessly interpret what they hear. But neither party, unless a professional linguist, is likely to offer more than a rudimentary account of the shared grammar which makes it possible for them to do it. Further, though both production and reception are technically faultless, neither the utterance or its interpretation are necessarily clear, unambiguous, free of connotation, incontestable. Even those who use their native tongue best – novelists, poets and playwrights – produce famously ambiguous and contestable utterances, and are notoriously bad at explaining what their works mean; and literary critics, whose very job description it is to say what they mean, are notoriously good at disagreeing about it. But, clearly, this is not to say that works of literature are devoid of meaning.

This is important here. In the wedding ceremony various semiotic languages are present: the verbal 'text', in both its relatively fixed liturgical aspect and relatively fluid celebratory aspect, and the 'scenography' of spatial organization, movement, colour and plastic form. Through these it is obvious that the ritualistic, though wholly non-mimetic, shares a significatory domain with the aesthetic, specifically with its dramaturgical sub-set.

Finally, in the context of weddings, the notion of dramaturgy is useful since its concern is with the form of literary fiction which repudiates interpretation through the intentional fallacy. Whatever the playwright's intention may be, performance is necessarily a collaborative event. It involves any number of people, each with a specialized function and particular perspective (literally as well as conceptually: actors never see their own performances, nor do they see from the auditorium the performances of their fellows in the same scene). So the act of performance immediately takes us some distance from any intended meaning on the part of the author; which is not at all the same as to say that it is meaningless.

But, one may object, presumably the artistic director knows what the whole thing means? As an experienced theatre director, I doubt it very much. When not purely pragmatic, production judgements are routinely made on the basis of whether it 'looks nice', 'feels right', and the actors are comfortable

Ritual Structure and the Dramaturgy of Food

with it; and thereafter (we hope) on the basis of pattern, coherence, repeated and developed image. That, likewise, can be observed in ritual, and is what this paper tries to analyse, with particular reference to ritual food. I am comfortable with the idea that meaning may be both allusive and elusive, performative and constitutive, connotative as well as denotative, and even, ultimately, sub-liminal; especially in a ritual which so strongly privileges thresholds.

So much for methodology. Substantively, the dramatic fiction is no bad model for an event which contains enough polite fictions to construct an average-sized airport novel.

A few examples: 'Who giveth this woman?' The only honest answer is, 'Well, I suppose she does really' (fortunately the bride's father is released from the outright lie by the fact that the script – the 1662 *Book of Common Prayer* – does not give him any lines). Then, as we all know, the bride's white dress stands for purity, and specifically for her virginity. Statistically, in 1999, this is a metaphor that cannot be cashed and everybody knows it.[3] Finally, even in 1999, I understand, there are young women who are daffy enough to promise to obey their husband. They will not, of course; and probably never did, even in 1662 or, for that matter, 1549.

All these little examples are dependent upon a big, over-arching, polite fiction, the ceremony itself. No offence is intended to practising Christians; but it can be observed that, in many cases, the wedding service as described might (without too much exaggeration) be characterized as a religious ceremony conducted by an agnostic on behalf of two atheists. This is only to say that ritual is normative (in sociological terms) or ideological (in political); and, from either perspective, rhetorical in its discourse. What it is not is an account, accurate in every detail, of either the material circumstances or a metaphysical reality. Yet, paradoxically, despite its palpable fictions, it is a powerful mechanism of the reorganization of those material circumstances on the foundation of a metaphysical reality.

How it does this, through its studied ambiguity and paradoxes, and specifically the part that food plays in that, is the subject here. The food in question is what is traditionally called the wedding-'breakfast' – though given that even the Roman Catholic church has in our lifetime relaxed its prohibition of eating before communion, that phrase is a graceful anachronism. That is, the meal served at the wedding reception, and particularly the wedding-cake.

Ritual Structure and the Dramaturgy of Food

Figure 2. This design dates from the 1880s when it was used by E.S. & A. Robinson, packaging manufacturers of Bristol. However, it reflects fashions current in the 1850s. A happy group is shown at the first cutting of a single (untiered) bride-cake, decorated with white icing.

Before examining these in detail, a brief word about the approach taken here. First, whilst historical considerations have been kept in mind, no account has been taken of them, unless in passing. Rather, the convention of the ethnographic present has been adopted in treating the English wedding ceremony in the second half of the twentieth century as a structural and dramaturgical paradigm. In any case, another paper in this volume deals with aspects of the history, as does Dr Charsley's erudite and challenging book. Second, and by the same token, the numerous (and probably increasing) variations in practice (including permitted liturgical choice) have been largely disregarded in favour of the grand generalization.[4]

Third, in discussing food, the concern here is as much with its appearance, order and distribution as content; and as much with its correspondences with other aspects of the event as its intrinsic qualities. The analytical perspectives derive, in the main, from Van Gennep's classic synoptic work of 1909,[5] which outlined the fundamental tripartite diachronic structure of the *rite de passage*: *séparation/passage/aggrégation* (separation/transition/incorporation); and from Lévi-Strauss's paradigmatic structuralism, principally in his 'Short Treatise on Culinary Anthropology' (originally 1968).[6] In addition, the charm of Berthold Brecht's ironic economism is irresistible:

> What must be shown here is the exhibition of the bride, of her carnality, at the moment of final withdrawal from circulation, that is, at the time when supply must cease, demand must once again be driven to the peak. The bride being generally desired, the bridegroom thereupon 'sweeps the board'.[7]

Brecht's joke need not be taken too literally: he is, after all, commenting on a scene in one of his own plays, the *Dreigroschenoper*, not on any actual or ideal wedding ceremony; but in it one can recognize that he has pointed us to something important, which ties in immediately to the thinking of Van Gennep and Lévi-Strauss. Namely, in the dramatic narrative of a wedding, the central character is undoubtedly the heroine. Whilst both parties are equally consenting to and implicated in the event and its repercussions, legally as well as morally, and while the groom has a few more lines of script ('with this ring I thee wed' etc.), the emphasis is in all other respects upon the bride. She arrives last (traditionally, a little late, to keep everybody waiting – a high-status gesture), and proceeds up the nave to solemn music, accompanied by not less than two attendants. She is also subject to comments on how beautiful she looks: 'radiant' is the common term, though one never hears the bridegroom described as preternaturally handsome. Conventionally, the wedding day is described as 'her day'; she is the receiver of a gift of precious metal from and is explicitly the object of worship by her bridegroom; she is herself a 'gift' from one man to another. Above all, she is wearing that fantastic dress.

Let me concentrate on the latter, because in due course I shall argue that it is homologous to the wedding-cake. I am not the first to be struck by this thought. In a whimsically anecdotal passage, Dr Charsley refers to it as having come to him while dozing on a train. His fully woken self, however, rapidly dismisses the notion on the grounds that, 'no such reading [of identity] would be culturally possible.'[8] On the basis of the dramaturgical, and by all means more diffuse, understanding of the generation of meaning outlined earlier, I am inclined to disagree.

First, whatever one thinks of the popular aetiology 'White=Virgin' (which, in a literal sense, is understandably regarded as irrelevant by most brides and most wedding guests), what is certain is that the dress is, in Peirce's terms,[9] powerfully indexical; as a sign, it is marked to the point of being uniquely individuated – and it is a serious social solecism for an adult female guest to wear white at another woman's wedding.[10] At its most tritely obvious, the dress loudly says 'This is the bride'; at its slightly less obvious, it says that this is the first time that this woman has been a bride, and in principle the last – which is also to say that she will only ever be the bride of this man on her right as surely as she will only ever be the daughter of that man on her left.

What else can be said about it? To put it in the form of a rhetorical question: what young woman, under other circumstances, spends (or has spent for her) more than she has ever spent before or will again on a dress she will wear only once? That alone shows how important it is, and how important she is in it. Incidentally, she is probably also carrying a bouquet which, though manifesting other colours, will also tend to emphasize white; or optionally a prayer book or Bible and, if so, it will be bound in white; and either (especially the bouquet) may have lucky charms attached to it, usually in the form of pasteboard horseshoes or bells in silver (another 'radiant' colour), which are gifts from members of her female peer group or small children within her extended family.

In Van Gennep's terms, clearly, this is a liminal costume. It is worn during the period between separation and re-incorporation. The former takes her from the state of betrothal; from all but a few representatives of her peer group of unmarried girls, from all men other than close kin, and from any illicit relationship which might have existed with her husband-to-be (even if she has been cohabiting with him, she is likely to have withdrawn continently to the parental home the night before her wedding). The latter re-incorporates her into adult society as a married woman jointly hosting, with her husband, their first dinner-party. The dress is worn until the couple retire from the reception to change into their 'going away outfits'. She was helped into it by her mother, sisters, female friends; she will be helped out of it by her new husband. All this is simple enough: a liminal costume for a liminal state (even the terminology is liminal: bride and groom are applicable for a few hours at most, and are customarily and formally supplanted, to general applause, by the groom's reference, in his speech of thanks, to his wife).

What of the groom? While she is dressed to kill in some more-or-less baroque confection, he stands there in his (frequently hired) black or grey morning coat or lounge suit equivalent, looking smart by all means, but in no way visually distinguishable from his own best man, the bride's father or, in principle, any other adult male present. His costume is marked only in so far as it is the normal formal male attire for a ceremonial occasion; and *ipso facto* it carries with it no popular aetiology of its significance, and specifically no reflection on his sexual status, actual or ideological. Semiotically, in contrast to his bride's outfit, his carries no special weight at all. By all means, his liminal situation is marked in other ways: his stag party, his prompt arrival (with his best man) to greet guests as they arrive at church, his early move to a special position where he can be seen by all and see nobody but his best man sitting beside him. But as dramatic statements, these are not in the same league.

We shall, I suggest, find something analogous when we look at the wedding breakfast, particularly in contrast to the wedding-cake. Before we leave the matter of costume, one last observation on colours. I have characterized the groom's costume as non-individuated. This is not to say that the groom may not individuate himself: I have personally seen a groom looking very dashing in a suit of dark green velvet, and it is not unknown recently (in a fashion development that I think takes us back to the eighteenth century)[11] for the groom to mimic the white garments of his bride. While the latter, like the white car with white-clad chauffeur which has become rather fashionable over the last couple of decades, raises cognitive issues that want more thought than there is space for here, the general truth is that, while the groom may individuate himself, he is not socially individuated. His dress is, given general conventions of formality, a matter of personal taste and subject to no constraint. Nor can he complain if somebody else shows up in green velvet (especially not in the early 1970s, which is the period that the example derives from).

The bride's dress, however, is thickly hedged about with protocol, specifically governing colour (there is more freedom regarding style, though modesty is on the whole preferred). Most obviously, if she does not wear white, it is difficult for her to avoid the inference that she is making a statement, and will set tongues clucking.[12] But further, let her try and introduce green or grey (even as a trimming), and it will not be just her granny who disapprovingly voices: 'Don't wear green/It's not fit to be seen,' or 'Marry in grey/You'll be a widow some day,' (which is statistically probable in any case). Even if they do not know the rhymes – and they probably do – they will assure her that it is, in some undefined sense, unlucky. Black, as the colour of mourning, is unthinkable; though apparently perfectly all right for all males of whatever age (as, indeed, is the classic grey morning coat or sober grey lounge-suit), and indeed for female guests (though bridesmaids dressed in black appear to be unknown). Red and yellow, even as decorative trimming, likewise seem to fall outside the range of acceptable colours.[13] Blue, conversely, is obligatory, but in a special sense: 'Something old, something new/Something borrowed, something blue'. In practice, the blue element is almost invariably hidden, and likely to be seen in the first instance only by her attendants and, subsequently, by her husband – or, of course, by all and sundry if she has colluded with that important ritual specialist, the photographer, in arranging a garter-shot.

In considering the wedding-cake, and its possible homology with the wedding dress, it will be important to have in mind the appearance of that extraordinary, radiant, white-clad figure, whose very size (obligatorily at really grand weddings) is magnified by a big skirt and several feet of train; and the other colours, or absence of them, that surround it, including pre-eminently the resolutely unmarked colour of the bridegroom. It would appear that, unlike her, he risks no pollution from colours; which is a vivid expression of the rather surprising fact that, just when we might expect symmetry, we get asymmetry. Of this more later; but, immediately, the wedding-breakfast.

Leaving aside its utilitarian and general social function in the domain of entertaining guests, it has, in this context, a very particular function which belongs to its place in the order of events. Structurally, the whole reception phase of the wedding belongs to Van Gennep's final segment, *aggrégation* or re-incorporation. The first move in this phase is when, having undertaken the legal formalities in the vestry, the couple re-emerge and process down the nave towards the west door. Assuming that the bride remains on the groom's left (as is usually the case in my observation – though, interestingly, nobody tells them to do this), the couple have inverted their previous spatial relationship: she is now to the (ecclesiastical) south, and hence nearer to the groom's family and guests; he to the north and hence nearer to her family and guests. The reorientation of social space is emphasized by the order of progress

Ritual Structure and the Dramaturgy of Food

following, in which, typically, the bride's father accompanies the groom's mother and vice versa, the best man accompanies the (chief) bridesmaid; and so on until the procession dissolves into a cheerful, chattering mêlée as the guests on both sides file out of their pews and mingle in no fixed order.

Thereafter, commemorative photographs and video recordings having been made, the bride and groom depart for the place of reception before any guest should arrive; there, they greet and thank the guests as they arrive. It is their first formal action as husband and wife (though those words have not yet been publicly used in a secular context) and, as such, constitutes their re-incorporation into society, but under a new rubric of role and status (note the inversion of word order: from the ephemeral 'bride and groom' to the permanent 'man/husband and wife'). This is emphasized in various ways, both solemn and comic, during the subsequent feasting, and notably by the speeches, which anecdotally relate the story of the girl who has become a woman and the boy who has become a man; enact the public role of the man who speaks and the woman who remains silent; and refer, through humorous and mildly obscene traditional formulae, to the impending wedding night (a secular parody of what the prayer-book text has earlier, just as explicitly and with great lyrical beauty, placed within a sacred frame).

Of the feast itself, two major points draw attention: first, that it may take two forms: a 'sit-down meal', typically of three courses, which anchors the guests spatially, according to a place-setting that mixes the two parties; or a 'buffet' which allows them to circulate, so that in principle the same end is achieved rather more anarchically. Of these two modes it need only be said, firstly, that both are entirely consistent with more general habits of entertaining, as one might logically expect of the phase of *aggrégation*; and secondly, that their only difference, structurally, is one of emphasis. The sit-down meal echoes, metonymically, the tripartite structure of the whole ritual, while the buffet, equally metonymically, refers specifically to the *aggrégation* phase, in that it is increasingly secular and informal. Alcohol and tobacco tend to emphasize this distinction further: the dispensation and use of both narcotics are relatively controlled during the sit-down meal, relatively uncontrolled during the buffet.

Both modes are consistent with general habits of entertaining, but there is little sign that, in either case, the participants have any particular preoccupation with the matter. People interested in food might regret that contemporary wedding menus show no sign of culinary specialization; for

Ritual Structure and the Dramaturgy of Food

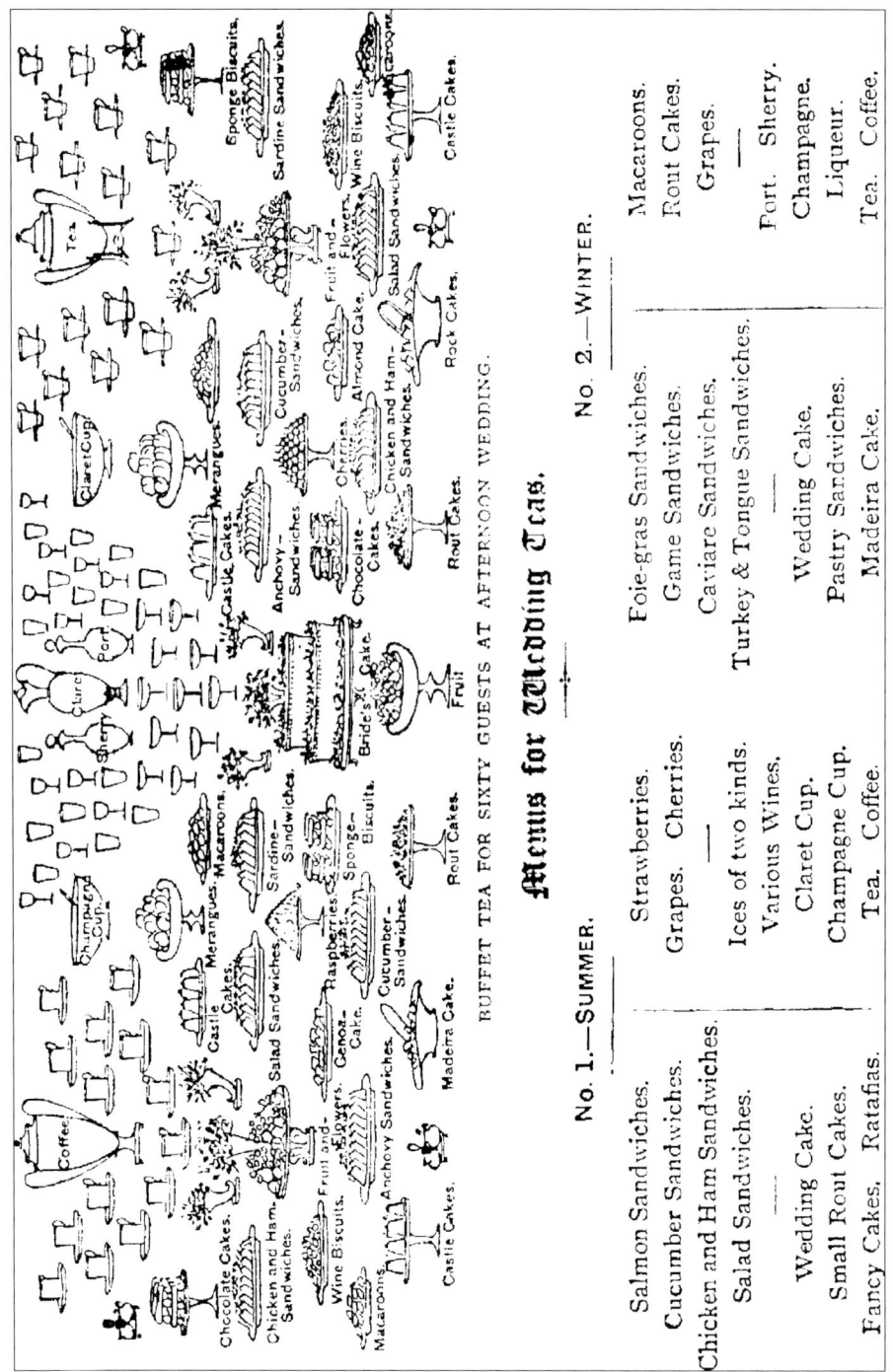

Figure 3. An illustration, taken from the 1901 edition of Isabella Beeton's Household Management, *depicting the arrangement and components of a buffet wedding tea.*

the participants, it would appear, the matter is one of virtual indifference.[14] Qualitatively (assuming that the wedding breakfast has been professionally catered for, which it almost invariably is), most of them probably cook better themselves, and could certainly eat better in a modest local Italian or Asian restaurant. In short, what the meal communicates and constitutes is something quite other than its standing as cuisine.

What it communicates and constitutes is normality, as against the highly abnormal behaviours of the separative and transitional phases of the ritual. If the matter is looked at from the other end – not, that is from the perspective of the ostensibly grand marriage feast but from that of the ostensibly humdrum round of family meals and casual entertainment – it becomes clearer. As Mary Douglas has argued:

> If food is treated as a code, the messages it encodes will be found in the pattern of social relations being expressed... The smallest, meanest meal metonymically figures the structure of the grandest...[and] admission to even the simplest meal incorporates our guest unwittingly into the pattern of solid Sunday dinners, Christmases, and the gamut of life cycle celebrations.[15]

A wedding breakfast has a difficult balance to maintain: it must be obviously celebratory (sparkling wine features) and at the same time non-threatening. At least in principle provided by the bride's parents, it must not seem in any way imposing or competitive, since, again in principle, at some point, the groom's parents are obliged (under normal social practice) to reciprocate; and, from a utilitarian point of view, it has to please everybody.

One final observation about the wedding breakfast, before considering the *pièce de résistance*, the cake: where the content of the meal is concerned, a contrast may be observed. In his 'Short Treatise', in elaborating his basic opposition between the Raw and the Cooked as homologous with the opposition between Nature and Culture, Lévi-Strauss draws up a 'culinary triangle', in which, semiotically, he contrasts roasting, boiling and smoking as methods of cooking. For present purposes, the matter of smoking is of little importance: canapés of smoked salmon are not unknown at wedding buffets, but they occupy no privileged position. The contrast between roasting and boiling, however, is of interest. It is, he proposes, fourfold.

Firstly, roasting, since the only mediator between the raw food and the fire is air, tends towards nature – which is emphasized by the fact that roasting 'is compatible with incomplete cooking, this incompleteness even being a sought-after effect in our West European societies',[16] whereas boiling, which has two mediators – liquid and an enclosing vessel – tends towards culture, which is emphasized by the incompatibility of boiling with incomplete cooking.

Secondly, boiling, a mode of 'endo-cookery', is associated with family food (notably where meat is concerned), and roasting, a mode of 'exo-cookery', with the entertainment of strangers, and with festive usage more generally.

Thirdly, boiling, as a conservative mode of cooking, is associated with frugality; whereas roasting, as a wasteful mode, is associated with extravagance.

Finally, and more speculatively, boiling is associated with relatively democratic and roasting with relatively plutocratic political structures.

Leaving aside that what the British call 'roasting' is in practice usually baking (which is a function of technology and of its definitionally higher level of enculturation, that is, greater distance from nature), the application of this fourfold contrast to our two forms of wedding breakfast is intriguing. Empirically, the main course of the sit-down meal usually consists of something roasted, whereas the centre-piece of the buffet is highly likely to be cold poached salmon or cold boiled ham, or both. Conversely, the roast meat will be accompanied by boiled vegetables dressed in heated butter, which is about as cultural as you get, while the salmon or ham will sit alongside raw vegetables, not to mention, in the case of salmon, an emulsion of raw egg and unheated oil and vinegar, which is about as natural as you get (at least in our culture where, on the whole, raw meat or fish is not favoured). So there is obviously a desire for complementarity; but the emphasis is different. Paradoxically, the more formal arrangement privileges nature, and the less formal culture.

It is possible that the paradox is satisfactorily accounted for by Strauss's second and third criteria (if not his more speculative fourth). Equally, it is possible that it derives from the contrasting applications of the metonymic trope: that the roast, standing as it does in the second position of three, mimics the second position ('transition', the 'liminal' position) of Van Gennep's scheme, as being neither quite the one thing nor the other; whereas the ham or salmon, as fully enculturated dishes presented in an open-ended, voluntary sequence (there is nothing to stop guests picking at the remains of the ham after they have had their strawberries and cream), reflect the consolidation of the day's event in its final phase.

Ritual Structure and the Dramaturgy of Food

Finally, the cake. In one sense, Douglas's point about metonymy applies again: a wedding-cake is only by degree different from other celebratory or indeed everyday[17] fruit-cakes in our tradition. Nevertheless, the difference of degree is substantial. First, a wedding-cake is obligatory, whereas Christmas-cakes are merely customary, and birthday-cakes tend quietly to disappear as people get older (until they get very old). Second, its architectural construction is far more elaborate than that of any other celebratory cake (it is frequently multi-tiered). Third, its ingredients and décor are at least as extravagant as those of any other cake, and generally more so. Fourth, it is not merely signed (so often are birthday-cakes), it bears two names; and only the baptismal names – the bride, let us not forget, is still in her wedding dress, and therefore still between identifying herself by her father's name or by her husband's.

Then, when we look not just at what it is as a confection, but at what is done with it, we are confronted with a difference not of degree, but of kind. First, it is cut by bride and groom conjointly, using the same knife; which is a unique event in our culture; people simply do not, otherwise, jointly cut food with a single knife (unless, twenty-five, forty, or fifty years on, they are re-enacting what they did on their wedding day). Second, it is then properly divided by professionals (or other adepts) and not only served to the guests but packed in little white boxes, often decorated, again, with silver bells or horseshoes, for postal distribution to family and friends unable to be present.[18]

So, if formally speaking the wedding-cake is metonymic of fruit-cakes – even if it is the *ne plus ultra* – functionally it seems to have properties which are actually or virtually unique to it. To determine what those are, it might be worth looking a little more closely at its formal properties. Let us begin with colour. The obvious feature is that, like the wedding-dress, the wedding-cake is essentially white (including modish shades like ivory). Additional colours, which are invariably restricted in number, range from silver, either as edible sugar decoration or inedible cardboard iconography, through dilute versions of the three primary colours, to (what appears to be a recent commercial trend) somewhat stronger, but still mixed, colours such as cerise, orange, and so forth. Generally strong colours are avoided: coffee and chocolate icing, both commonplace of professional confectionery, are never seen on wedding-cakes. And green is, in my experience, conspicuous by its absence. Dr Charsley, whose field work was undertaken chiefly in Scotland, encountered it as a confectioner's colour, which may suggest that English and

Scottish traditions are divergent in this respect; he does, however, clearly imply that, even in Scotland, it is not a popular colour.[19] Interestingly, Dr Neale, in reporting on her impressively detailed field work in Leeds, refers to a green-trimmed cake, but specifically in the context of its having provoked the satirical disapproval of the wedding guests.[20] The similar absence of grey is probably wholly utilitarian: apart from the skin of fish (which in our culture most people do not care for), it is not a common food colour, and I am unaware of its use in confectionery generally.

In short, the permissible range of colours for the cake is, for all practical purposes, the same as the permissible range for the wedding-dress (including its trim). And it is worth noting that, until recently (and still to quite a large extent), the dress of bridesmaids has been dominated by pastel shades, to their despair. It is as if those strong primary colours, especially the optically forward red, with its strong local cultural connotations of romantic love, danger and explicit sexuality, become acceptable only at low saturation. Even the lucky colour, blue, is unlikely to appear in its darker hues. And the fourth primitive or *Urfarbe*,[21] green, is on the whole avoided; possibly because it is perceived as adulterated blue (on the same principle, perhaps, that grey is adulterated white).

So much for colour. What about plastic form? Here, I confess, I am on even shakier ground, since my argument may be over-reliant on recent trends in fashion. Be that as it may: ethnography is nothing if not contemporary; and it may be that a given fashion has merely made manifest what was covertly there all along. Thus, since the wedding of the late Lady Diana Spencer, whose dress was apparently designed by the Emanuels to look like a wedding-cake, and which remains a very influential style to this day, it has been difficult not to ask oneself the chicken-and-egg question: does the girl look like the cake, or the cake like the girl?[22] The question is intrinsically unanswerable. That cake and dress belong in the same iconic domain, and that the cake pursues and reinforces the dramaturgy of the dress, is manifest.

If we scrutinize that action, the ritual cutting of the cake, especially in the light of Van Gennep's account of the incidence of cutting and breaking within *rites de passage* generally, what do we see? That, often with the assistance of a ritual specialist who will direct the couple to plunge the knife into warm water, the ornate white crust is broken by bride and groom in physical collaboration; and the product is freely distributed, not only to those present, but to a wider community. At the risk of labouring the point: loving sex is a free gift, and so too are children. The action is at once indexical and symbolic, not only of an existing condition (between the couple), but of a future potential which will continue long after those two have undergone the last rite of passage that any of us undergoes. Or, in Lévi-Strauss's terms, a classic example of endo-cooking (the cake is baked in a container within a container) fulfils the event's most obvious exo-function (it is distributed not only to those present but to those absent).

It is a complex little event, then, in that, for two people to cut a grandly iced cake with the same knife is actually quite difficult (hence the ritual specialist's assistance), yet they do not rehearse it. And utilitarian reasons will not serve to answer this. Could it be cost in money or effort? Hardly. It would cost relatively little to produce a single, plainly-iced cake for them to practise on – much less than is routinely expended by the groom's father on a single round of drinks – and any bride's aunt would knock one up overnight, were she asked. The point is, I suggest, that they have not practised. Actually, in our culture, people do not jointly use the same knife; ideologically, in our culture, people do not have sex until they are married. That in fact they do and possibly always have is a private matter. To marry, and therefore to invite witness to the nature of the relationship, is a public one; and one that is discussed verbally in perfectly explicit terms, within both the solemnity of the liturgy and the anarchic (and for the most part highly formulaic) comedy of the best man's speech and reading of the telegrams.

Which raises two final points: first, regarding the relationship of bride and groom within the ritual, which this essay has so far characterized as asymmetrical; second, regarding the ritual's final phase. To take the second first: there is no religious or legal requirement for a wedding reception, much less a wedding-cake. Yet the reception, the third phase of the ritual, takes up more time, on the day itself, than phases one and two put together, and almost certainly more money: useful indices, both, of its social importance. I suggest this is to be accounted for by a celebrated gloss on Van Gennep, published by Victor Turner.[23] This states that the tripartite structure is not simply a succession of stages identical in tone and substance: but that it encapsulates a locally variable dialectic, not only between Nature and Culture, but between two human perceptions of society, which Turner calls societas and communitas.

To simplify: in our contemporary protestant Christian English wedding, the move is explicitly from anarchy to order (in a very high and metaphysically sanctioned degree) and back to anarchy. And, within that move, the deictic and symbolic asymmetry of bride and groom is resolved into the symmetry of husband and wife: the liminal emphasis on the bride as the object of a contract between two men, and on the control of her sexuality, is resolved through the emphasis upon the two of them as partners by mutuality. This is achieved at once grossly, by the best man's traditional verbal clowning, which makes no distinction between bride and groom/husband and wife: 'Today's the day, tonight's the night/We've shot the stork, so you're all right,' and, subtly and delicately, by the cutting of the cake (by the way, any theatre director who achieved this effect would rightly be regarded as a genius). Finally, note that this is achieved not in isolation, but as the culmination of the wedding breakfast, itself the culmination of a complex process of the dramatizing of known human relationships, both particular and general. The importance of the wedding breakfast is precisely that it is humdrum; the importance of the wedding-cake is precisely that it is not.

It is obvious that many ambiguities and paradoxes remain unresolved in this discussion. Even given the space and time to address them more closely, some would probably remain unresolved. As Lévi-Strauss says, in concluding his 'Treatise':

> cooking is a language through which … society unconsciously reveals its structure, unless – just as unconsciously – it resigns itself to using the medium to express its contradictions.[24]

And that is, among other things, where we would need to return to history.

Ritual Structure and the Dramaturgy of Food

Notes

1. Simon R. Charsley, 'Interpretation and Custom: The Case of the Wedding Cake', in *Man*, n.s. 22 (1987) 93–110; and *Wedding Cakes and Cultural History* (Routledge, 1992). See also his 1988 article 'The Wedding Cake: History and Meanings', in *Folklore* 99: ii, pp. 232–241.
2. Brenda Anne Neale, *Getting Married: An Ethnographic and Bibliographic Study*, 2 vols. (PhD Thesis, University of Leeds, 1985) particularly Ch. 2, 'Theoretical Developments' and Ch. 3, 'Urban Ritual Studies'. I am grateful to Dr Neale for permission to refer to her thesis, which is under restricted access.
3. Nor is this necessarily a recent phenomenon. The study of parish registers, some decades ago, showed that a substantial minority of seventeenth-century brides were pregnant on their wedding days, a phenomenon probably associated with formal betrothal. See Peter Laslett *The World we Have Lost* (Methuen, 1965) especially Ch. 6, 'Personal Discipline and Social Survival'; and Lawrence Stone, *The Family, Sex and Marriage in England 1500–1800* (Weidenfeld and Nicholson, 1977).
4. In discussion following the presentation of this paper at the Leeds Symposium, Val Mars kindly drew my attention to the 'anomic wedding', viz., the forms of wedding which break any or all of the conventions, discussed here, of the 'solemnisation of matrimony'. I was vaguely aware of these (via newspaper accounts of weddings under water, secular ceremonies organized by community-theatre companies such as Welfare State International, and so forth), but I did not previously know that they had achieved scholarly categorization. I am grateful to Ms Mars for this information; which would be crucial to any fully conceived sociology of my subject, to which this essay has no pretensions.
5. *Les Rites de Passage*, trans. Monika B. Visedom and Gabrielle L. Caffee, *The Rites of Passage* (Routledge and Kegan Paul, 1960). (Rather literal, but the phrase has stuck, so congratulations to the translators.)
6. As a chapter in his *L'Origine des Manières de Table, Mythologiques*, Tome 3 (Paris: Librairie Plon) trans. John Weightman and Doreen Weightman, *The Origin of Table Manners: Introduction to a Science of Mythology* 3 (Jonathan Cape, 1978) pp. 471–495.
7. Desmond I. Vesey (trans.), 'Notes on the Threepenny Opera', in *Three German Plays* (Harmondsworth: Penguin Books, 1963), p. 232. (Originally published in the *Versuchehefte* 3, 1930.)
8. 'Interpretation and Custom', pp. 105–107.
9. Charles Sanders Pierce, *Collected Papers* (Cambridge, Mass: Harvard University Press, 1931–58) especially Vol. 2.
10. As the late Princess Grace of Monaco discovered to her cost when a guest at the wedding of the (then) Princess Anne to Captain Mark Phillips. Even that rather radical journalist Terry Coleman, writing for that then rather radical newspaper *The Guardian* (if my memory serves me), denounced her temerity in trying to 'upstage an English princess on her wedding-day.' It has recently come to my notice that the singer 'Scary Spice' has solved the problem by the radical solution of 'ordering everyone to wear white,' Rosie Millard (14.6.1999); 'Here comes the bride,' *The Guardian: G2*, p. 4. Is this girl-power or another anomic wedding?
11. See Peter Linebaugh, *The London Hanged: Crime and Civil Society in the Eighteenth Century* (Allen Lane, 1991).
12. Dr Neale (1985) provides concrete evidence of this, with reference to the colour pink as being locally interpreted as a sign of the bride's sexual experience. Most strikingly, one of her informants had elected to wear pink on her wedding day precisely because she was not a virgin: vol. 2, p. 360.
13. I have, incidentally, come across proverbial rhymes against these too, but they seem not to have the wide currency of those against green and grey; and I have never heard it said that these colours are 'unlucky'; nevertheless, they seem not to be in the palette.

14. I think it is important here that we remind ourselves of the wise words of that wisest of all cultural analysts, the late Raymond Williams in 1965: 'It is...not a question of relating the art to the society, but of studying all the activities and their interrelations, without any concession of priority to any one of them we may choose to abstract': *The Long Revolution* (Harmondsworth: Pelican Books, 1961) 1st edition, p. 62.
15. Mary Douglas, *Implicit Meanings: Essays in Anthropology* (Routledge and Kegan Paul, 1975) especially 'Deciphering a Meal', pp. 249–275 (originally 1972). My quotation, though verbatim, is not a piece of continuous prose, but a summary conflation of her views which I trust I have not misrepresented.
16. Lévi-Strauss (1978) pp. 482–3.
17. I do not know if this is a term in general use. I have it from my Selby-born mother-in-law who used it of the lightly textured fruit-cakes she baked for routine domestic consumption, in distinction from the more complex ceremonial cakes. I mention it only because I suspect that the language of cooking deserves more attention, both dialectally and semantically.
18. The only other instance of that which I have heard of concerns the christening cake, which I suspect to be derivative.
19. Charsley (1987) p. 96.
20. Neale (1985) vol. 2, p. 465.
21. Marshall Sahlins, 'Colors and Cultures', in *Semiotica* 16: 1 (The Hague: Mouton, 1976) pp. 1–22.
22. At least one cheap vulgarian of a television commentator (I do not recall the name or channel) evidently thought that the first was true. When that (with hindsight) sad young woman emerged from the car before St Paul's, and the nation got its first glimpse of the dress, he commented: 'She is gift-wrapped.'
23. Victor Turner, *The Ritual Process* (Routledge and Kegan Paul, 1969).
24. Lévi-Strauss (1978) p. 495.

CHAPTER TWO
BRIDECUP AND CAKE:
THE CEREMONIAL FOOD AND DRINK OF THE BRIDAL PROCESSION

Ivan Day

I sing of May-poles, Hock-carts, Wassails, Wakes,
Of Bride-grooms, Brides, and of their Bridall-cakes.[1]

Popular traditions of food and drink associated with weddings – throwing rice, cutting the cake and the champagne toast for the happy couple – are familiar throughout twentieth-century Britain. Like many other customs surrounding celebration foods, it is vaguely assumed that these practices have emerged from ancient folk beliefs or arcane religious rituals. For understandable reasons, most of our traditional foods have been handed down without the convenient attachment of a reliable history. Their potency as symbols of continuous custom and antiquity ensures that popular myth has frequently been used to explain their origins. For instance, it is popularly believed that the architectural character of the wedding-cake was inspired by the tiered spire of St Bride's church in Fleet Street, a romantic explanation that is almost certainly fanciful.

Fallacies such as this date back to nineteenth-century antiquarians and writers of popular histories, who tended to explain the past through anecdote, rather than by critical appraisal of historical fact. At a time when parallels were being drawn between the British Empire and that of the Romans, many were preoccupied with finding classical precedents for our national customs. For instance, the late nineteenth-century antiquary J.C. Jeaffreson rather simplistically argued that the bride-cake represented an unbroken tradition dating back to the Roman wedding ritual, which involved the breaking of a cake of grape must and flour over the bride's head.[2]

In *Wedding Cakes and Cultural History*, the social anthropologist Dr Simon Charsley reviews many of the customs that have crystallized around the wedding-cake and expresses much caution about accepting such beliefs.

Summarizing these difficulties, he states:

> Myth looks to the past to explain whatever is perceived to be important in the present; history seeks, like the anthropologist in another country, to understand the differentness of the past on its own terms.[3]

Dr Charsley's book is essential reading for anyone embarking on a study of the historical problems associated with the evolution of foods linked with rites of passage. He sees the royal-iced wedding-cake of our own times as an example of cultural marooning, 'a European *pièce montée* petrified into a new age.' He compares its survival to that of the Scottish haggis and oatcake, which 'represent in the modern world dishes which are ancient, were once widespread, but which have been maintained in Scotland as tastes and technology moved on elsewhere.'[4]

This essay is concerned chiefly with the development of the wedding-cake in the early-modern period, before it became an architectural caprice of royal icing and sugar paste. It deals mainly with a type of cake that would be unrecognizable to a modern wedding guest and attempts to place it into the context of a long-forgotten wedding day ritual. It also seeks to clarify the history of some other ceremonial foods and drinks associated with the post-Reformation English wedding and bridal feast. Most ritual foods of this kind, with their strong connections with religion and folklore, are so redolent of myth that, despite the warnings of contemporary authorities like Dr Charsley, it is often impossible (and sometimes unwise) to separate them from the beliefs which apparently gave them their birth.

Figure 4. A seventeenth-century woodcut showing the attendants on a bride sporting sprigs of rosemary tied to their arms.

Bridecup and Cake

The ritual role of cakes in British calendar and agricultural festivities has an ancient pedigree. There was a time when we marked the progress of our year with cakes for Twelfthtide, Shrove Tuesday, Mothering Sunday, Whitsuntide, the important celebrations around harvest-time and All-Souls day, not just Christmas and Easter. For many hundreds of years important milestones in our personal lives have also been traditionally honoured by cakes – our christening and funeral as well as our wedding.

The earliest known English record of a cake or loaf used in a ritual context occurs in a complex twelfth-century remedy, written in Old English and Latin, designed 'to amend thine acres if they wax not well.'[5] In this remarkable charm the Earth Mother is invoked in a powerful hymn:

Erce! Erce! Erce!
Mother Earth
May the Almighty grant thee.
The Eternal Lord,
Acres waxing
With sprouts wantoning,
Fertile, brisk creations,
The rural crops,
And the broad
Crops of barley

Then after repeatedly chanting, '*Crescite et multiplicamini et replete terram,*' a broad loaf, baked with meal of every kind, kneaded with milk and holy water, was buried under the first furrow cut by the plough.

The manuscript in the British Library which contains this ancient benediction[6] appears to have been written by an early twelfth-century scribe, who almost certainly copied it from an earlier source. The hymn to the Mother Goddess is also known from several Continental sources, the earliest of which dates from the sixth century and contains strong Stoic and Neo-Platonic elements. It probably dates from late antiquity.[7] However, the burial of a sacramental loaf is only described in the Old English text.

The multi-grain nature of the sacrificial loaf is reminiscent of the 'porridges' of many types of seed that have been found in the digestive tracts of Iron Age bog burial victims in Denmark.[8] What appears, at first glance, to be a straightforward Anglo-Saxon charm is, perhaps, a complex fusion of pre-Christian, classical and early Christian elements.

The implied durability of cake burial in England does seem to point to a genuine survival of this particular folk custom, rather than a self-conscious salvage of ancient superstition. Sacrificial use of a loaf or cake to encourage the fertility of the coming season's crops appears to have had a remarkable longevity. Even today, some West Country apple orchard wassailing rites feature cake burials. In the late nineteenth century, Mrs A.B. Gomme collected the following Shrovetide variant of the *Orange and Lemons* rhyme, in Northamptonshire:

> Pancakes and fritters,
> Says the bells of St. Peters:
> Where must we fry 'em?
> Says the bells of Cold Higham:
> In yonder land thurrow [furrow]
> Says the bells of Wellingborough.[9]

This image of ploughboys burying pancakes in the Northamptonshire fields in honour of Ceres (or some other long-forgotten local incarnation of the grain goddess) is a romantic one. It would be tempting to assume that the wedding-cake, with its obvious associations with fecundity, is somehow related to these ancient loaves linked to agricultural fertility rituals.[10]

Whatever the true origins of the wedding-cake, it is impossible to escape from its powerful connections with both sexual and pastoral fecundity. Louis de Gaya, author of *Matrimonial Ceremonies Displayed* (published in London in 1748), describes the eighteenth-century Jewish wedding ceremony:

> The Bridegroom walks three Times round his Bride and takes her by the Hand, then the Company throw Corn upon them with that saying in the Scripture Phrase 'Crescite et Multiplicamini, Encrease and Multiply.'

In a footnote, the author offers an interpretation:

> this Strewing of Corn upon their Heads, was to betoken their Worldly Encrease in Children and Substance: and doubtless was the Origin of the Bride Cakes amongst the Christians.[11]

The use of the same scriptural allusion in the Jewish wedding ceremony and the Anglo-Saxon charm is striking. However, the true origins of 'the bride-cakes among the Christians' are probably much more firmly rooted in an important feature of the nuptial mass than in native folk religion or the diffusion of Judaic or Roman wedding traditions, though elements of all these seem to be part of the picture.

At weddings in pre-Reformation Europe it was the practice to carry wine and bread in a procession to the church for the priest's blessing. The ceremony itself usually ended with prayers based on the scriptural references to Christ's Miracle of the Marriage Feast of Cana. After these the bread was distributed among the guests with the cup of blessed wine.

In Catholic countries, this custom continued until quite recently. The author of *Matrimonial Ceremonies Displayed* tells us that in eighteenth-century France:

> the Procession ends with a Servant of the Bridegroom, or Bride, who carries the Bread in one Hand, and the Wine in the other, which the new married are obliged to present in the Church. After the Nuptial Benediction, the new married assist at the Holy Sacrifice of the Mass, each holding a lighted Candle with which they go to the Crucifix, and present Bread and Wine to the Priest, according to the ancient Usage of the Church.[12]

Pre-Reformation service books, such as the fifteenth-century *Rathen Manual*, indicate that a variation on this practice took place at the end of the nuptial mass in Britain:

> After mass there shall be blessed some bread and wine or any pleasant drink in a vessel, and they shall taste it in the name of the Lord: Bless O Lord this bread and this drink as Thou didst bless the five loaves in the desert and the six water pots in Cana of Galilee, that all who taste therof may be healthy, sober and undefiled.[13]

Although the true sacrament of communion was dropped from the wedding service in England at the time of the Reformation, the custom of blessing bread (or more specifically cakes) and wine, provided by the bride and groom, appears to have persisted well into the seventeenth century. During the preparations for his daughter's wedding, in Thomas Dekker's play *Satiro-mastix* (first published 1602), Sir Quintilian Shorthose tells his servant, Peter Flash, 'when we are at Church bring wine and cakes.'[14]

Although a cake is mentioned, in a list of suggested foods suitable for an aristocratic wedding feast, in the instructional manual *Ffor to serve a Lord* of c.1500, it is not until the Elizabethan period that bride-cakes are actually described, and then usually as an important feature of wedding processions.[15] In order to understand the part the cake itself played in this context, it will be necessary to examine the other traditions of these processionals in some detail.

The earliest reference to a nuptial cortège is in a letter from Robert Laneham, which describes an entertainment provided by the Earl of Leicester for Queen Elizabeth when she visited Kenilworth Castle in 1575. As part of the festivities, a comical masque based on a bridal procession was given by a group of players in the castle tilting yard. In Laneham's own words:

> a solem brydeale of a proper coopl waz appointed: set in order in the tyltyard. Fyrst, all the bold bacherlarz of the parish, sutablie every wight with hiz blue buckram bridelace upon a braunch of green broom (caus rosemary is skant thear) tyed on his leaft arme (for a that syde lyez the heart. Then, three pretty puzels az bright az a breast of bacon, of a thirtie yeere old a pees, that carried three speciall spisecakes of a bushel of wheat, (they had it out of my Lord's backhouse,) before the Bryde: Syzely, with set countenauns, and lips so demurely simpring, az it had been a Mare cropping of a thistl. After theez, a loovely loober woortz, freklfaced, red headed, cleen trust in his dooblet and hiz hoze, taken vp now in deed by commision, for that he waz so loth to cum forward, for reverens (belike) of hiz nu cut canvas dooblet; and woold by hiz good will have been but a gazer, but found too bee a meet actor for his offis: that waz, to bear the bridecup, foormed of a sweet sucket barrell, a faire turnd foot set too it, all seemly bysylvered and parcell gilt, adourned with a beautiful braunch of broom, gayly begilded for rosemary: from which, too brode brydelaces of red and yeloo buckeram begilded, and galauntly streaming by such wind as thear waz for hee carried it aloft:) This gentl cupbearer yet had his freckled fiznemy sumwhat vnhappily infested, az hee went by the byzy flyez, that floct about the bride cup for the sweetnes of the sucket that it savored on: but hee, like a tall fello, withstood their mallis stoutly (see what manhood may do!), bet them away, kild them by scores, stood to hiz charge, and marched on in good orde.[16]

This comical performance assumes total familiarity, on the part of the audience, with the customary rituals of a wedding, otherwise the farcical humour of the situation would not have been fully understood. It implies that bride maids struggling with great spice-cakes and cupbearers holding aloft bride-cups of wine adorned with rosemary must have been common sights in Elizabethan England. Laneham's own enjoyment of the ironic humour of the event particularly comes across in his description of the rustic red-haired cupbearer being attacked by the flies. The role of the usher who carried the wine to be blessed in the church was a solemn one, as was that of the maids who carried the loaves. The cupbearer at Kenilworth, with his 'freckled fiznemy' and the thirty year old 'puzels', with their lips simpering like those of a mare cropping a thistle, turn the customary solemnity of a wedding feast into a riot of fun. These rustics seem to be performing a spoof on an Elizabethan society wedding. Surely the 'special spise cakes', made from a whole bushel of wheat, and a silver and gilt bride-cup would have been expensive props at a commonplace country wedding. The fact that the bride-cup (at a real noble wedding it would have been a valuable silver-gilt vessel) was improvised from a barrel for storing fruits in syrup adds more ironic humour to the situation.

That these rituals were customary at the weddings of the wealthy are borne out by another description of a similar nuptial procession, in Thomas Deloney's *The Pleasant History of John Winchcombe* which, though first published in 1626, was probably written in the late sixteenth century. Deloney's account refers to a wedding which is alleged to have taken place in the early sixteenth century:

> The Bryde being attyred in a gowne of sheepes russet, and a kyrtle of fine woosted, her head attyred with a billiment of gold, and her haire as yeallow as gold, hanging downe behinde her, which was curiously combed and pleated, according to the manner in those dayes: shee was led to churche betweene two sweete boyes, with Bride-laces and Rosemary tied about their silken sleeves; the one of them was sonne to Sir Thomas Parry, the other to Sir Francis Hungerford. Then there was a fair Bride-cup of silver and gilt carried before her: wherin was a goodly branch of Rosemary gilded very faire, hung about with silken ribands of all colours: next was there a noyse of Musicians that played all the way before her: after her came all of the chiefest maydens of the Country, some bearing great Bride Cakes, and some Garlands of wheate finely gilded, and so she past into church.[17]

As well as bride-cakes, rosemary was an important feature at Elizabethan and Stuart Weddings. This herb was thought to aid the memory and, as a symbol of remembrance, was worn at funerals, but was also carried at weddings because it was considered to have strong cordial properties. In a sermon of 1607, entitled *A Marriage Present*, the preacher Roger Haket explains the significance of the plant for the bride and groom:

> Another property of the rosemary is, it affects the heart. Let this rosmarinus, this flower of men, ensigne of your wisdom, love and loyaltie, be carried not only in your hands, but in your hearts and heads.[18]

It was carried in the bridal procession at the wedding of Sir Quintilian Shorthose's daughter in Dekker's play, which also refers to another Tudor wedding custom, the distribution of perfumed gloves among the guests:

> More rosemary and gloves, gloves, gloves Choose gentlemen, Ladyes put on soft skins upon the skins of softer hands; so, so: Come Mistress Bride take your place, the olde men first, and then the Batchelors; Maydes with the Bride, Widdows and wives together, the Priests at Church, tis time that we march ther.[19]

In the opening scene of this play, just before sunrise, two unmarried gentlewomen are strewing the path between the bride's house with flowers. One of them, whose youth is well behind, is in an ill humour, so her companion chides her, 'Truth I think thou mournest, because thou hast mist thy tyme.' In a skilful play on words, she then reverses the usually joyful emblematic significance of the wedding procession props in order to mirror her companion's self-pitying reflections on her unmarried state:

> the Silver Ewers weepe most pittiful Rosewater: five or six payre of the white innocent wedding gloves, did in my sight choose rather to be torne in peaces than to be drawne on, and like this Rosemary (a fatall hearbe) this deade-mans nose-gay, has crept in amongst these flowers to decke th' nuisable coarse of the Brides Maydenhead.[20]

In a wedding scene in Ben Jonson's play *The Tale of a Tub* (1640) the bride maids present the groom, on his first appearance, with 'rosemary beribboned'; while in Deloney's account, cited above, the rosemary sprig in the bride-cup is also gilded, a wedding practice which Robert Herrick refers to in his two line verse, *To Rosemary, and Baies*:

> My wooing's ended; now my weddings neere;
> When Gloves are giving, Guilded be you there.[21]

Gilded rosemary was not just a feature of wedding processions, but also a decorative garnish used during this period to embellish festival foods, such as brawn.[22] In the accounts for a dinner of 1566, for the Draper's Company, a painter called Yong (probably Young) was paid 36s 8d, 'for gilding of Brawn, Jelly & Sturgeon'.[23] Like the rosemary it adorned, gold was also considered to be a powerful cordial medicine with beneficial effects on the heart. For this reason it was frequently included in cordial waters, such as *aureum potabile* and usquebaugh.[24]

At weddings the rosemary bough was also dipped in rose-water before it was carried to church – the ewers mentioned in Dekker's work were probably used for this purpose. Ewers were also a favourite gift at aristocratic weddings. A beautiful gold ewer and basin were given by James I as a present to his daughter Princess Elizabeth and the Elector Palatine at their wedding in 1613. Both objects, which survive in the Royal Collection, are engraved with the Elector Palatine's arms.[25] The practice of scenting the rosemary is also described in Beaumont and Fletcher's play *The Scornful Lady* (1609):

> Were the gloves bought and given, the licence come,
> Were the Rosemary branches dipt, and all
> The Hipochrists and cakes eate and drunke off.[26]

Rose-water was thought 'to fortify the heart and revive all the Spirits, Natural, Vital and Animal.'[27] Roses were one of the four Galenic cordial flowers – the others were borage, bugloss and violets which, according to Haket, were the favourite strewing herbs at weddings.

In addition to the rosemary and bride-cakes, gilded garlands or ears of wheat seem to have frequently been carried by the bride maids. Of all the folk customs associated with marriage, this and the playing of loud music were the ones most frowned upon by the Puritan reformers. In 1572, the Presbyterian John Field complained:

> Women, contrary to the rule of the Apostle, come, and are suffered to come, bare-headed, with bagpipes and fiddlers before them, to disturb the congregation, and that they must come in at the great door of the church else all is marred (with divers other heathenish toys in sundry countries, as carrying of wheat-sheaves on their heads and casting of corn, with a number of suchlike, whereby they make rather a May-game of marriage than a holy institution of God).[28]

Figure 5. Joris Hoefnagel, 'A Wedding Fête at Bermondsey', c. 1569–1571. (Reproduction by courtesy of the Marquess of Salisbury.)

Thomas Moufet tells us more about the custom:

> When the bride comes from Church, they are wont to cast Wheat upon her head; and when the Bride and Bridegroom return home, one presents them with a pot of Butter, in presaging plenty and abundance of all good things.[29]

Despite Puritan attacks on this practice, the casting of wheat survived for a long time in country districts, as did that other token offering to the grain goddess, the strewing of flowers 'on the starry way to church'. In Henry Rowe's poem, *The Happy Village* (1796), we are told:

> The wheaten ear was scatter'd near the porch,
> The Green Bloom blossom'd strew'd the way to church.[30]

Other than some other minor references in plays and historical accounts, the sources cited above are among the few written records we have of the protocol of Tudor weddings. By amalgamating features from all of them, it is possible to propose how the colourful and noisy events of an upper-class nuptial procession would have unfolded.

Early in the morning, her maids would have strewn the way from the bride's house to the church with flowers. Then, just before the procession set off, the guests were given white, scented gloves as presents and the rosemary sprigs were dipped in rose-water. The procession was led by a cupbearer or 'bryde leader', who held aloft a silver-gilt bride-cup adorned with a branch of gilt rosemary tied with coloured ribbons. Behind the cupbearer were the old men of the family, followed by the musicians, and behind them the bride, accompanied by young pages wearing bride laces and rosemary on their left arms. Behind the bride were her maids, some carrying great spice-cakes and others gilded garlands of wheat. Family widows and married women completed the wedding train. During the course of the nuptial service the priest blessed the cup of wine and the bride-cakes. When the wedding was over, the bride's head was scattered with wheat at the church porch and the procession reformed to march to the place of the feast or bridal (from Old English *brȳd-ealu* – literally, bride ale).

In addition to the written sources cited above, a remarkable visual record of these long-lost customs has also survived. The Flemish miniaturist Joris Hoefnagel (1542– after 1600) recorded the principal features of a wedding of this kind during a brief residence in London between 1569 and 1571.[31] Hoefnagel lived among a small community of Flemish refugees on the South Bank and the scene of his painting is probably set in the village of Bermondsey, close to where he lived. Although food historians have frequently alluded to this work, its significance to the history of the wedding-cake has never been discussed (see figures 1, frontispiece, and 5, opposite).

On the right hand side of the painting a bridal procession, just like those described by Laneham, Deloney and Dekker, is emerging from the church-yard, probably that of St Mary Magdalene. Two young women and two young men (all four carrying great bride-cakes) lead the procession. They are followed by two fiddlers and a bride leader, who is bearing aloft what appears to be a gilt ewer decorated with a very large branch of rosemary tied with many tiny red and white 'bryde knots'. This resplendent nosegay is also adorned with two larger 'bryde laces' consisting of white and red ribbons, 'galauntly streaming by such wind as thear waz,' just as in Laneham's description. These are inscribed with mottos, or perhaps the names of the bride and groom, though it is not possible to read the actual words. Tiny gilded flags painted with what seem to be armorial designs also embellish the rosemary. Following the cupbearer are the principal guests, who are all carrying the customary white, scented gloves. Although the way to the church is not strewn with flowers, the damask tablecloth in the feasting house is decked with scattered blossoms.

A great bridal feast is being prepared in the kitchen. Careful scrutiny of the area behind the servery reveals the spectacular embellishments of what are almost certainly grand sallets, the opening dishes of the feast. A solitary turn-spit rotates the spits on the cob irons of the great raised roasting range. The close proximity of the four cake-bearers to the kitchen and the pasty-like form of the cakes have led some authorities to assume that they are waiters carrying great pies or venison pasties.[32] Venison pasties did frequently feature at wedding feasts and were a favourite marriage gift. In 1547 the London draper Otwell Johnson sent six large venison pasties to Calais for his brother Richard's marriage feast.[33] But the evidence cited above, and the fact that they are walking from the direction of the church rather than the kitchen, confirm that these enormous pastries are indeed the great bride-cakes of a nuptial procession. Hoefnagel's extraordinary skills as a miniaturist also help confirm this hypothesis, since careful examination of the crusts reveals meticulously painted currants erupting through the pastry.

The pasty-like form of these cakes is easily explained. In 1655, the first published recipe for a great cake specifically baked for a wedding appeared in *The Queen's Closet Open'd*, a collection of recipes from aristocratic sources, allegedly compiled for Queen Henrietta Maria. This was '*The Countess of Rutlands Receipt for making the rare Banbury Cake, which was so much praised at her Daughters (the Right Honourable the Lady Chaworths) Wedding*' (the full recipe can be found on p. 143). Fundamentally this is a rich plum cake enclosed in an outer pastry case, rather like a giant Banbury or Eccles cake. To help the dough rise, the recipe instructs us to prick the top and to 'cut the side round about with a Knife an inch deep.'[34] These features can clearly be seen on Hoefnagel's cakes.

After baking, the Countess's cake weighs in at over thirty pounds. Allowing for an average seventeenth-century oven door width of about eighteen inches, it needs to be made in elliptical form in order to easily get it in and out of the oven. (I have made a number of these cakes using the full quantities suggested in the recipe and baked them in a wood-fired oven. The final dimensions of all have been about thirty by sixteen by five inches; their shape and size closely match those of the cakes depicted in Hoefnagel's painting.)

A cake of these dimensions is a heavy, ungainly object and Hoefnagel has shown us how they were carried in a sling-like napkin, tied around the usher's neck, and supported by the hands from the side. This stance also allows the beauty of the cakes to be admired as they are paraded before the bystanders. The great size of the cakes, and the fact that three or four of them were baked at a time, suggest a very large number of guests. It is likely that when the cake was broken, pieces were distributed throughout the community. Early wedding feasts were celebrations to which everyone was welcome. Bride-cakes at marriages lower down the social scale were probably much smaller, whilst at royal weddings delicate wafers instead of cakes were distributed among the guests. At the wedding of James I's daughter Elizabeth to the Elector Palatine in 1613 there was,

> in conclusion, a joy pronounced by the King and Queen, and seconded with congratulations of the Lords there present, which crowned with draughts of Ippocras out of a great golden bowle, as an health to the prosperity of the marriage (began by the Prince Palatine and answered by the Princess). After which were served up, by six or seven Barons, as many bowles filled with wafers, so much of that work was consummate.[35]

Although there is a seventy-five year gap between Hoefnagel's painting and the Countess's recipe, the form of her cake agrees perfectly with those in the painting. Many of the folk customs associated with the early wedding processional were probably long forgotten by the early 1650s when Lady Charworth's wedding took place. Nevertheless, it would seem that the great bride-cake of the Tudor period managed to survive the religious and social upheavals of the seventeenth century, including the Civil War.

These cakes were apparently eaten at the end of the bridal feast, just as wedding-cakes are today, and therefore may have been a major feature of the banquet or sweet after course. The Wiltshire antiquary John Aubrey (1626–97) recollected the bride-cakes of his childhood:

> When I was a little boy (before the Civill Warres) I have seen (according to the custome then) the Bryde and Bride-groome kisse over the Bride-cakes

at the Table: it was about the latter end of dinner: and the cakes were layd one upon another, like the picture of the Sew bread in the old Bibles.[36]

Rich in butter and strongly scented with rose-water, musk and ambergris (the same perfumes used to scent wedding gloves), the Countess's cake, like most of the cakes of this period, was raised with ale barm and was really an enriched fruit loaf. Its outer crust of dough was probably designed to protect the currants in the filling from burning and also suggests it may have evolved from a much simpler hearthcake. Though it makes quite good eating, it is rather heavy and bready in texture. Appreciating this helps shed light on the nuances of meaning in Herrick's poem *The Bride-cake*:

> This day my Julia thou must make
> For Mistresse Bride, the wedding Cake:
> Knead but the Dow and it will be
> To paste of Almonds turn'd by thee:
> Or kisse it thou, but once, or twice,
> And for the Bride-Cake ther'l be Spice.[37]

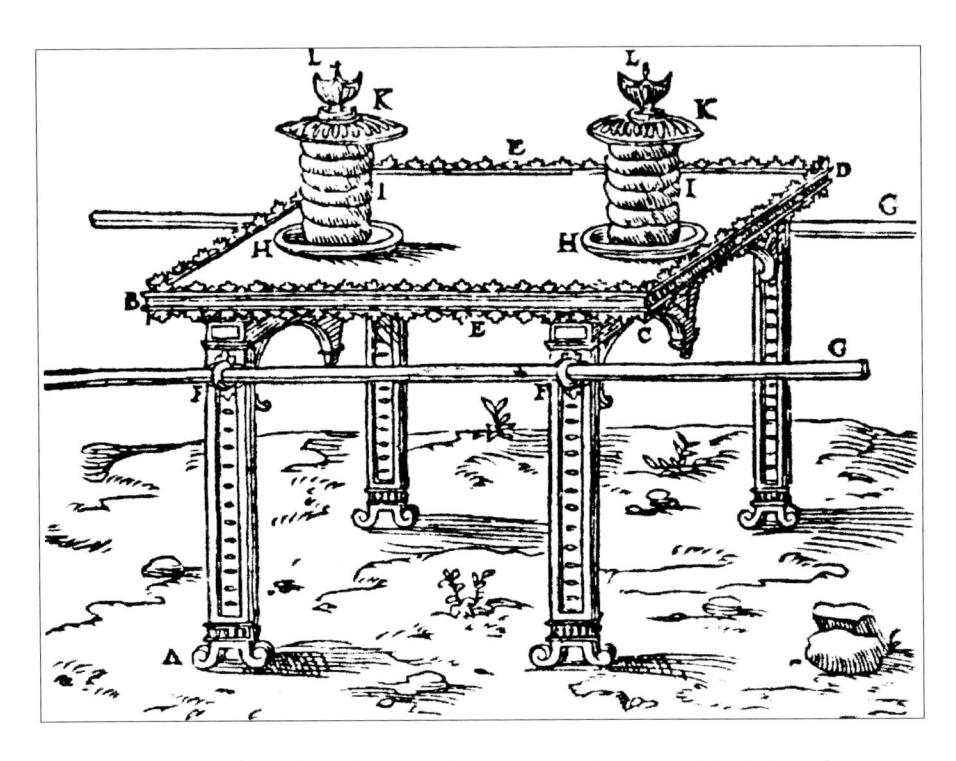

Figure 6. Shew bread, from the Geneva Bible, 1650, as referred to by John Aubrey, above.

Paste of almonds was one of the most celebrated and expensive luxury foods of the period. It was used to make the large decorative centrepieces for the banquet course, known as marchpanes. By the magic touch of her hand, Herrick's mistress Julia transforms the heavy dough of the rustic bride-cake into extravagant marchpane paste. (In another verse, in which he dotes on this extraordinary woman, Herrick has her lending extra perfume to an already 'richly redolant' pomander bracelet – simply by wearing it on her wrist!)

Combined with sugar icing, almond paste (sometimes called 'love' or 'matrimony') is of course an essential ingredient of the modern wedding-cake. Bride-cake recipes that include it start to appear in cookery books in the second half of the eighteenth century, though it is likely the practice was well established much earlier. The earliest printed recipe was that of the Manchester confectioner Elizabeth Raffald (1769) whose instructions differ considerably from those given for the barm-leavened cake of Lady Charworth's wedding.[38] Raffald's bride-cake uses beaten egg as a raising agent and is cooked in a paper-lined garth or wooden hoop. It is not encased in a dough shell like the earlier form of bride-cake, but, after baking, is covered with a layer of almond paste followed by one of sugar icing. It is clearly the model for the wedding-cake of our own times.

C. Anne Wilson thinks the highly decorative wedding-cake so familiar today may have developed from an eventual fusion of the great plum cake and the iced marchpane with its sugar paste embellishments. Charsley feels that Wilson's hypothesis is overstated, but there is some evidence to support her theory.[39]

Decorated marchpanes certainly featured at wedding banquets. In 1552 Sir William Petre purchased one hundred of them, 'wrought with no small curiositie,' for a wedding at Ingatestone Hall in Essex.[40] Moreover, marchpanes identical to those described in sixteenth- and seventeenth-century English cookery texts were eaten in the Low Countries at wedding feasts and are frequently depicted in still-life paintings. Interestingly, these were usually embellished with a sprig of rosemary decorated with gilded lozenges. Clara Peeters (*fl.* 1600–20), in a painting of *c.*1615, depicts one on a table covered with other foods emblematic of married love – oysters, cotagnata in scatoline [boxed quince preserve] and a gimblette or jumble in the form of a true lover's knot. The iconographical significance of rosemary and gold to married love seems to have been appreciated far beyond the shores of Britain (see figures 7 and 8, below).[41]

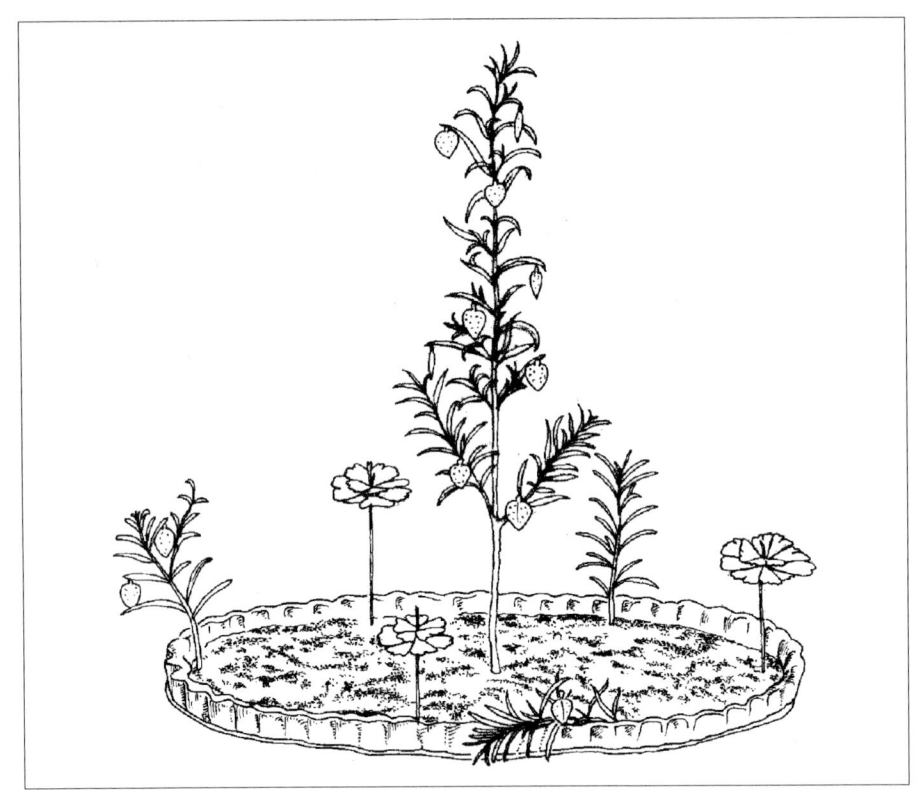

Figure 7. A marchpane, embellished with sprigs of rosemary decorated with gilded lozenges, ornamented with sugar-paste clove gillyflowers or carnations, as depicted in a still life by the Dutch painter Clara Peeters (fl. 1600–20), in c.1615. The marchpane's surface was scattered with coloured comfits, like our modern hundreds-and-thousands.

However, there is only one isolated piece of evidence in the seventeenth century to show that plum cakes were decorated at this period with the elaborate sugar decorations usually reserved for marchpanes. This is in the 1674 edition of *The Queen-like Closet* by Hannah Woolley, and is not for a bride-cake.[42] Her detailed directions are for making a complex, edible, table centrepiece based on a foundation of 'good thick Plum Cake'. She assures her readers, 'Do not take this for a simple fancy, for I assure you, it is the very same that I taught to a young Gentlewoman to give for a Present to a person of quality.' Woolley's cake, which she calls 'a Rock in Sweetmeats' is a Restoration reincarnation of a medieval *soteltie*. Covering the cake is a fantasy mountain landscape of 'ill-favoured stones' made of bisket, macaroons, rough almond cakes, candied fruit and just about every kind of comfit and sweetmeat made in the seventeenth century. Sugar plate snakes, snails and worms, as well as a marchpane peacock stuck with 'some right Feathers gummed on with Gum Arabick', populate this edible mountain. The full text of her recipe is given on p. 144.

In *The Whole Duty of a Woman* (London, 1701), a small chapbook that includes a few cookery recipes, the anonymous author describes the adornments used to decorate a *Cake-Royal with Comfits*: 'Your small Toys made of Sugar, in the Shape of Birds, Beasts, Flowers &c. are made of melted Sugar in Rose-water cast in Moulds, and Gilded or Painted afterwards at Discretion.'[43] It is not until the 1790s that we again hear of plum cakes being embellished with sugar decorations. In 1795 the Scottish cookery author Mrs Frazer gives these directions to decorate a Seed or Plumb cake in the second edition of *The Practice of Cookery*:

> If you choose to ornament your cake, put a crown in the middle, and other small fancy figures on the top, waving small shells up and down the sides of it, and putting a bunch of artificial flowers of different colours so as to stand within the crown; the crown, figures and shells are made of sugar paste, the flowers and leaves of different coloured paste, and the stalks of lemon peel. The three first are sold in the confectioners shops, and the others you can do yourselves according to fancy, after being taught to make pastes, and how to cut them.[44]

Though Mrs Frazer's instructions are not specifically for a bride-cake, it would seem that cakes for weddings were also decorated in this way; in the same year that her book was published, the Reverend James Woodforde recorded in his diary:

> Mr Custance sent us this Evening a large Piece of a fine wedding Cake sent from London to Mr C. on the Marriage of Miss Durrant (daughter of Lady Durrants) and Captain Swinfen of Swinfen-Hall in the county of Stafford, eldest Son of ――― Swinfen, Esq. Very curious devices on Top of the Cake…[45]

Numerous wooden confectioners' moulds from this period have survived for making crowns, figures and other devices from sugar paste. They are often in the form of a card or mosaic mould, a slab of wood carved in intaglio with a number of designs. The early nineteenth-century Edinburgh confectioner, J. Caird, tells us that, 'a board of various figures, such as leaves, flowers, trophies, etc.will cost about 3L.'[46] The best quality moulds were carved from

Figure 8. A jumble in the form of lovers' knot, as depicted in a still life by the Dutch painter Clara Peeters (fl. 1600–20), in c. 1615.

boxwood. In his *Treatise on Confectionery* of 1817, Joseph Bell, a Scarborough confectioner who once worked for the Prince of Wales, explains how sugar-paste baskets were made from mosaic moulds. He also gives the first English illustrations of decorated cakes, though none of these are bride-cakes and most are based on sponge cakes, what Caird calls 'diet loaves'. There are surviving wooden moulds to make some of the features that Bell illustrates, such as his Prince of Wales feathers, a star of the garter and sugar swans.[47]

A much earlier card mould, probably dating from the first quarter of the eighteenth century, survives in the Pinto Collection at the Museum of Science and Industry in Birmingham. This would have enabled a confectioner to construct a three-dimensional sugar-paste tester bed from the six different components carved on the mould. Edward Pinto, in his book about the collection, has suggested that this may have been used as an embellishment for a bride-cake.[48] Though he cites no evidence to support his argument, it is well known that similar sugar decorations, in the form of infants in cradles, were used to grace the tops of christening-cakes. The provenance of the mould is also unknown – it could quite easily be Dutch rather than English. However, the potency of the marriage bed as an emblem would have certainly made it an appropriate decoration for a bride-cake at a time when it was customary for the bride and groom to be put to bed by their family and friends. This public bedding of the bride came in for a great deal of criticism. In *Matrimonial Ceremonies Displayed* (1748) we are told:

All that Bustle and Stir that is so generally made at putting the Bride and Bridegroom to Bed, I think is very impertinent, and I might have added indecent too: For such a Hurry of People gaping and starring, and jesting, and jibing upon them, cannot but put them both into disorder and Confusion; and a Woman must have a very great State of Assurance, not to blush at so many disorderly Railleries.[49]

A rare insight into these 'disorderly railleries' is shown in Marcellus Laroon's drawing of 1722, in which he illustrates the custom of throwing the bride's stocking. This was one of many divination rituals associated with weddings. It is clearly explained in the anonymous poem *The Progress of Matrimony* (1733):

Then come all the younger folks in,
With ceremony throw the stocking
Backward, o'er head, in turn they toss'd it:
Till in sack-posset they had lost it.
Th' intent of flinging thus the hose
Is to hit him or her on the nose
Who hits the mark o'er the left shoulder
Must married be ere twelve month older.[50]

Aubrey is the earliest author to mention divination rituals of this kind. He describes how Wiltshire country girls made 'dumb cakes' from flour and egg white and placed them under their pillows, in the hope that they would dream of their future husbands.[51] In Henry Rowe's poem *The Happy Village* (1796) we are informed that very similar divination rituals were centred on the bride-cake itself:

The Wedding Cake now thro' the ring was led,
The Stocking thrown across the nuptial Bed.[52]

This refers to the custom of passing a small piece of cake through a wedding ring, as at a gentry wedding at Welford in Berkshire in 1770:

a profusion of bride Cake was placed ready for refreshment; & salvers of rich wine, & a gold Cup containing an excellent mixture, were handed round. The Bride and Bridegrooms healths were drunk, & pieces of cake were drawn properly thro' the wedding ring for the dreaming Emolument of many spinsters and Batchelors.[53]

Figure 9. In Robert May's The Accomplisht Cook *(1660), this figure for an 'extraordinary Pie, or a Bride Pie of several Compounds, being several distinct Pies on one Bottom', appears to show five pies stacked one on top of another.*

In later accounts of this superstition we learn that the bride held the wedding ring while the groom passed the piece of cake through it nine times in an obvious imitation of the act of coitus. Each piece was carefully sealed up in 'an envelope of fair writing paper' before it was placed under the pillow of the hopeful dreamer.[54] In the days leading up to the Welford wedding, the guests passed the time of day by stamping coats of arms on paper doilies. Although the Reverend Abdy does not offer an explanation for these, they were probably used for wrapping up the small pieces of cake used for divination.

According to the astrologers the wedding ring was worn on the third finger of the left hand because this finger was connected directly to the heart and was governed by Sol (the sun) whose metal was gold.[55] Reginald Scott in *The Discovery of Witchcraft* (1584) indicates that the magical powers of the ring were thought to cure various sexual problems. Among 'certain Popish and Magical cures, for them that are bewitched in their privities,' he cites a remedy which instructs the patient 'to piss through a wedding ring.'[56]

Rings used for divination purposes were also important features of pies served at Scottish penny weddings. Both Mrs Frazer (1791) and Mistress Margaret Dodds (1826) give recipes for bride pies which feature a glass ring embedded in a pastry lid ornamented with leaves, flowers and figures.[57] Caird tells us:

> when this is made in a tin shape, a glass ring put into the middle, covered, finely ornamented and baked, and turned out upon a dish, it

is named the bride's pye, from an old adage that the lady who gets the ring will be the first bride of the party.[58]

Anyone tucking into an earlier form of bride pie may have encountered a much more potent emblem of sexuality. In addition to an array of foods with aphrodisiac properties, such as cock stones, lambs stones and oysters, any wedding guests unfortunate enough to break into Robert May's extraordinary 'bride pye' of 1660, will have been surprised by:

> live birds, or a snake, which will seem strange to the beholders, which cut up the pie at the Table. This is only for a Wedding to pass away the time.[59]

This potent vision of the serpent Mother Eve's temptation was enclosed in the central pie of a complex arrangement, reminiscent of a knot garden made up of seventeen intricately shaped sections (see fig. 9). Eighteenth-century bride pie recipes such as that of Anne Peckham (1773) omitted the snake, but continued to include the cock stones and oysters.[60]

Another divination superstition that featured the wedding ring was focused round the wedding posset, referred to in the poem *The Progress of Matrimony* cited above. Posset was a comforting blend of alcohol, eggs, cream, sugar and spice, popular with all classes as a warming nightcap. While the wealthy fortified their possets with sack, lower down the social scale ale was the chosen form of alcohol. The custom of drinking the bride and groom's health in a draught of posset before they retired to bed seems to have emerged during the course of the seventeenth century. Frequently, a wedding ring was thrown into the posset pot and it was believed the first person to fish it out would be the next to marry. A full account of this and other wedding traditions associated with posset is given by Peter Brears in his paper, 'Wassail! Celebrations in Hot Ale'.[61]

It would appear this custom spread to the British colonies. The following recipe in verse was published in *The New York Gazette* on 13 February 1744:

Receipt for all Young Ladies that are going to be Married
To make
SACK-POSSET
From famed Barbadoes on the Western Main,
Fetch sugar half a pound; fetch sack from Spain
A pint; and from the Eastern Indian coast

Nutmeg, the glory of our Northern toast;
O'er flaming coals together let them heat
Till the all-conquering Sack dissolves the sweet.
O'er such another fire set eggs twice ten,
New born from foot of Cock and rump of Hen;
Stir them with steady hand, and conscience pricking,
To see the untimely fate of twenty chicken.
From shining shelf take down your brazen Skillet
A quart of milk from gentle cow will fill it:
When boiled and cooled, put milk and sack to egg,
Unite them firmly like the Triple League.
Then cover close, together let them dwell
Till Miss twice sing: You must not kiss and tell.
Each lad and lass snatch up their murderous spoon,
And fall on fiercely like a starved Dragoon.

The instructions to twice sing the popular song 'You must not kiss and tell' refers to the need to allow the posset to rest a short time. This allowed the custard layer on top to separate out from the alcoholic liquid. To keep the mixture warm, the posset pot was usually placed close to the fire, though one seventeenth-century source advises the kitchen maid to smother the posset pot between two cushions.[62] With the following remarkable exception (itself a classic example of what Charsley would call 'geographical marooning') posset is no longer used to toast the bride and groom at British weddings. This sole survivor of the practice is the Bride's Cog, a posset of hot ale, whisky, beaten eggs and sugar, still circulated at the end of wedding festivities in the Orkney Isles.

However, the tradition of serving posset at the end of the day, before the happy couple retired, needs to be separated from the custom of toasting the couple directly after the nuptial service. In the Tudor and Stuart periods, the chosen drink for this purpose was the spiced-wine hippocras or hipochrist – mentioned in Jonson's *Tale of a Tub* and served at Princess Elizabeth's wedding, in 1613, from a great golden bowl. Hippocras was a general-purpose celebration drink which was also imbibed at christenings. It probably derived its name from the *manicum hippocraticum* or apothecary's sleeve, a woollen jelly bag used to strain the spice particles from the wine. To make particularly clear hippocras, up to three *manica* were suspended one above the other. In addition, milk was frequently poured into the hippocras gyle (wine and spice mixture) as a fining. The tiny curds that formed when the milk reacted to the acid wine blocked the mesh and improved the efficiency of the sleeve, though it slowed down the filtration process.

Although recipes for hippocras appear in contemporary cookery texts (often in the section on 'banquetting stuffe'), most of the drink consumed at weddings was probably purchased from vintners. Another luxury drink frequently used to toast the couple was muskadine, or muscaden, a compound wine related to hippocras, but flavoured with coriander and cypress chips. Recipes for both drinks appear in a small treatise first published in 1682 for professional vintners and wine coopers. The anonymous author of this work tells us:

> I shall conclude with two common compounded wines, Muscaden and Hippocras, the former usually made with 30 gallons of Cute (which is Wine boyled to the consumption of half) to a Butt of wine. Or the Lees and droppings boyl'd and clarified; its flavour is made of coriander seeds prepared and shavings of Cyprus wood. Some instead of Cute, make it of Sugar, Molosses and Honey, or mix them with the Cute. This following is an Hippocras of my own making, and the best I have ever tasted.
>
> Take of Cardamoms, Carpobalsamum of each half an ounce, Coriander seeds prepared, Nutmegs, Ginger, of each 2 Ounces, Cloves 2 drachms; bruise and infuse them forty eight hours in Zerez and White wine, of each a Gallon, often stirring them, then add thereto of Milk three pints, strain through an Hippocras Bag, and sweeten it with a pound of Sugar-Candy.[63]

In the seventeenth century this particular hippocras must have been the equivalent of today's finest vintage champagne. What made it so special was the inclusion of the extremely scarce flavouring *carpobalsamum* (the dried fruits of a rare and unidentified balsam tree). According to the French herbalist Pomet this spice was only obtainable from a solitary tree growing in the Caliph's garden in Cairo, which was constantly guarded by janisseries.[64] Other professional hippocras gyle recipes in the 1682 treatise include spices which had long vanished from the kitchen such as long pepper, calamus, andores, cubebs, gallingal, cantherum and grains of paradise. If *carpobalsamum* and other rare spices were the choice ingredients of the better kinds of hippocras, luxury forms of muskadine were scented with a special perfume called a 'pearl', made from orris, *calamus aromaticus*, musk and civet.

Recipes for hippocras and muskadine disappeared from English cookery texts during the course of the eighteenth century. Nevertheless, the passing round of 'a gold Cup containing an excellent mixture' appears to have survived, as at the Welford wedding of 1770. However, by this time the custom had become purely secular. The 'blessing of bread and wine or any pleasant drink in a vessel' of the pre-Reformation nuptial mass had been long forgotten, as had the perfumed bride-cup of the Tudor procession with its flurry of rosemary and ribbons.

Despite these changes, one ancient custom continued unabated. This was the strewing of grain over the bride's head, though by the eighteenth century the wheat of tradition was likely to have been joined or replaced by comfits. These sugar-coated nuts and seeds became a universal feature of weddings throughout Europe from the Renaissance onwards. Their Italian name *confetti* was transferred in the nineteenth century to the small paper shapes we throw at modern weddings and carnivals.

Closely related to the strewing of wheat or comfits was the custom of breaking a cake over the bride's head. Despite Puritan disapproval, humanist preoccupations with antiquity during the sixteenth and seventeenth centuries may have encouraged this practice, with its powerful echoes of both ancient Judaic and Roman customs. Herrick refers to it in another poem devoted to Julia, this time to her churching:

> All Rites well ended, with faire auspice come
> (As to the breaking of a Bride-Cake) home:
> where ceremonious Hymen shall for thee
> Provide a second Epithalamie.[65]

No evidence for the breaking of the cake over the bride's head exists from the Tudor period, and it is not until the time of Herrick that we hear of it at all. Herrick's verse, with its constant use of antique poetical forms and classical allusions, does not necessarily reflect the actual folk practices of his day. His wassails, wakes and hock carts could just have easily taken place in Arcadia as in rural England. Aubrey mentions the practice in passing and makes a point by linking it with the ancient Roman custom.[66] Eighteenth-century accounts of bride-cake breaking are rather scant, or are in the context of fictional accounts and therefore not reliable.[67] However, there are a number of trustworthy reports of the practice from nineteenth-century folklorists, all from northern England or Scotland. The Reverend William Carr, a local historian from Craven in Yorkshire, cites one of the most interesting:

> The bridal party, after leaving the church, repair to a neighbouring inn, where a thin currant-cake, marked in squares, though not entirely cut through, is ready against the bride's arrival. Over her head is spread a clean linen napkin, the bride-groom standing behind the bride, breaks the cake over her head, which is thrown over her and scrambled for by the attendants.[68]

A variation on this procedure is reported from the Scottish Borders, though a piece of shortbread rather than a currant hearthcake is used to scatter on the bride's head.

> As the newly-married wife enters her new home on returning from the kirk, one of the oldest inhabitants of the neighbourhood, who has been stationed on the threshhold, throws a plateful of short-bread over her head, so that it falls outside. A scramble ensues, for it is deemed very fortunate to get a piece of the short-bread, and dreams of sweethearts attend its being placed under the pillow.[69]

This particular rite of passage, which took place on the threshold of the house, is reminiscent of the widespread grain- and comfit-throwing practices of other European countries. De Gaya, for instance, tells us that in eighteenth-century Poland, they:

> wash the bride's feet and sprinkle the bed with the water. They throw Wheat, Rye, Oats, Barley, Rice and Beans at the Doors, saying, That the Bride should never want any of these Grains if she continue devout in her Religion, and takes care of the Affairs of the Family.[70]

With its noisy music and comfit hurling, the type of bridal procession which wealthy eighteenth-century Portuguese colonists brought to distant Goa seems as colourful as its sixteenth-century English equivalent:

> When they are married they are brought home in some Order, with the sound of Trumpets, Cornets, and other musical Instruments, every one as they pass by throwing Flowers, sweet Waters and Confits upon them, which are gathered up by the Servants that wait on them.[71]

Bridecup and Cake

Modern weddings seem dull when compared to their ancient predecessors, but many of the associated folk customs endure, though usually in disguised form. Confetti has replaced the strewing of wheat and comfits and the cake is now cut rather than broken over the bride's head. Although a toast in champagne has substituted the bride-cup of hippocras, its ribbons still adorn the bridal bouquet. Even the white sash worn by the bride leader (as in Hoefnagel's painting) survives on the bridal limousine.

Although the great ritual cakes of the Elizabethan procession have long gone, the bride-cake has not changed much at all since the eighteenth century. At a time when it is possible to order one on the Internet, it is heartening to realize just how many hopes and aspirations this ancient mixture of flour, dried fruit and spice has symbolized for so many couples over so many centuries.

BRIDECUP AND CAKE

NOTES

1. Robert Herrick, *Hesperides* (1648).
2. J.C. Jeaffreson, *Brides and Bridals* (1882).
3. Simon Charsley, *Wedding Cakes and Cultural History* (Routledge, 1992), p. 29.
4. Charsley (1992), pp. 138–9.
5. Ms. Cott. Calig. A. vii., fol. 171 a. A translation of this charm is included in T.O. Cockayne, *Leechdoms, Wortcunning and Starcraft in Early England*, vol. I (1864-1866), pp. 398–405. The passages quoted here are from Cockayne's translation.
6. British Library Ms. Cott. Calig. A. vii., fol. 171 a.
7. Voss Leyden and R.Q.J. Heim in *Flecheisen's Jarhrb. F. klassische Philologie*, Supplementband 19 (Leipzig, 1892).
8. P.V. Glob, *The Bog People* (Faber and Faber, 1969).
9. A.B. Gomme, *The Traditional Games of England, Scotland and Ireland* (1894).
10. It is interesting to note that although no cake featured in the celebrations, the principal soteltie displayed at the wedding feast of Thomas Courteney, Earl of Devonshire in *c.* 1431 was an image of 'Ceruus' (presumably Ceres). MS. Harl. 279, in Thomas Austin (ed.), *Two Fifteenth Century Cookery Books* (Early English Text Society, 1888).
11. Louis de Gaya, *Matrimonial Ceremonies Display'd: wherein are exhibited, the various customs, odd pranks, whimsical tricks and surprizing practices of near one hundred different kingdoms. Collected from the papers of an old rich bawdy batchelor. To which is prefix'd, the comical adventures of Sir Harry Fitzgerald, who had seven wives, etc* (1748), p. 19. This work is a translation of *Cérémonies nuptiales* by Louis de Gaya.
12. de Gaya (1748), pp. 27 and 31.
13. D. McGregor (ed.), *The Rathen Manual*, (Aberdeen: Aberdeen Ecclesiological Society, 1905). Transactions IV, Special Issue.
14. Thomas Dekker, *Satiro-mastix. Or the Untrussing of the humorous poet* [i.e. Ben Jonson]. *As it hath bin presented publikely, by the Right Honorable, the Lord Chamberlaine his seruants; and priuately, by the Children of Paules, London* (1607).
15. In F.J. Furnival (ed.), *Early English Meals and Manners* (Early English Text Society, 1868).
16. Robert Laneham, *A letter: whearin, part of the entertainment vntoo the Queenz Maiesty, at Killingworth Castl, in Warwik Sheer, in this soomerz progress, 1575, iz signified: from a freend officer attendant in coourt, vntoo hiz fraend a citizen, and merchaunt of London* (1576). [Signed: R. L. Gent. Mercer, i.e. Robert Laneham.]
17. Thomas Deloney, *The Pleasant History of John Winchcombe* (1626).
18. Roger Haket, *A Marriage Present* (1607).
19. Dekker (1607). Recipes for scenting gloves are frequently offered in contemporary 'books of secrets'. Sir Hugh Platt (*Delights for Ladies*, 1609) gives complex instructions for scenting gloves with musk, informing us that gloves made from lamb's leather needed a slightly different treatment from those made from kid's skin or goat's skin. He also tells us that, 'Tenne graines of muske wil give a sufficient perfume to eight paire of gloves', p. 100.
20. Dekker (1607).
21. Herrick (1648).
22. Robert May, *The Accomplisht Cook* (1660).
23. Drapers' Company, Ms D.B.I. (1564–1602).
24. Ivan Day, *Cordial Waters, in Strength and Chearfulness. The John Towse collection of English tall cordial glasses* (Chippenham: Delomosne & Son, 1997).
25. Christopher Garabaldi, personal communication.
26. F. Beaumont and J. Fletcher, *The Scornful Lady* (1616).
27. William Salmon, *The New London Dispensatory* (1692).

28. John Field, *A View of Popish Abuses yet remaining in the English Church, for which the godly Ministers have refused to subscribe* (1572).
29. Thomas Mouffet, *Healths Improvement* (1633).
30. Henry Rowe, *The Happy Village* (1796).
31. E. Auerbach and C. Kingsley Adams, *Paintings and Sculpture at Hatfield House* (Constable, 1971).
32. Sara Paston-Williams, *The Art of Dining* (The National Trust, 1993), p. 113. See also Peter Brears, 'Pots for Potting', in C. Anne Wilson, *Waste Not, Want Not* (Edinburgh: Edinburgh University Press, 1989), pp. 33–4, 36.
33. Barbara Winchester, *Tudor Family Portrait* (Jonathan Cape, 1955).
34. The 1658 edition of *The Queen's Closet* is the first to correct a spelling mistake which occurs in the first edition of 1655. In the former, one is instructed to 'cut it in the midst of the sight round about with a knife an inch deep.' The 1658 clarifies this by replacing 'sight' with 'side'.
35. J. Nichols, *Progresses and Public Processions of James I* (1828).
36. John Aubrey, *The Remains of Gentilisme and Judaisme* (1687) reprinted J. Britten (ed.), in *The Publications of the Folk-Lore Society* IV (1881).
37. Herrick (1648).
38. Elizabeth Raffald, *The Experienced English Housekeeper* (1769).
39. C. Anne Wilson, *Food and Drink in Britain from the Stone Age to Recent Times* (Constable, 1973), pp. 270–1; and Charsley (1992), p. 67.
40. F.G. Emmison, *Tudor Food and Pastimes* (Benn, 1964).
41. See Peter Brown and Ivan Day, *Pleasures of the Table* (York: York Civic Trust, 1997), p. 55.
42. Hannah Woolley, *The Queen-like Closet* (1674), pp. 307–311.
43. Anon., *The Whole Duty of a Woman* (London, 1707) 4th edition, pp. 169–170. This work should not be confused with a much larger book of the same title published in London in 1737.
44. Mrs Frazer *The Practice of Cookery, Pastry, Confectionary, Pickling, Preserving, &c* (Edinburgh, 1795) second edition.
45. Reverend James Woodforde, *The Diary of a Country Parson* (1758–1802), ed. J. Beresford (Oxford University Press, 1978).
46. J. Caird, *The Complete Confectioner and Family Cook* (Leith, 1809).
47. The bride-cake in its later decorated form is really beyond the scope of this essay and the reader is referred to Dr Charsley's book for a fuller treatment of the history of the cake in the nineteenth and twentieth centuries.
48. Edward Pinto, *Treen and other wooden bygones* (Bell and Hyman, 1969), pp. 187–8.
49. de Gaya (1748), p. 42.
50. Anon., *The Progress of Matrimony* (1733).
51. Aubrey (1687). This custom survived into recent times. In North Yorkshire, in the twentieth century, a single girl, odd numbers or an even number such as 2, 4 or 8 girls would make Dumb Cake, composed of salt, flour and water, prepared and baked before the fire in silence on St Agnes' Eve (20 January); see Richard Blakeborough, *Yorkshire Wit, Character, Folklore and Customs* (Saltburn-by-the-Sea: W. Rapp, 1911) 2nd edition, p. 71. Elsewhere ingredients included soot or urine of the girls. A large flat cake was pressed out and each had to prick or draw on their initials. When it was baked each took her own piece to her room, walking backwards still in silence and without laughing. A piece of the cake under the pillow would bring dreams of the future husband (John Kightly, *The Perpetual Almanack*, Thames and Hudson, 1994), hence another name, 'dreaming cake'. A dreaming bannock in Scotland was to be made on All Hallows' E'en. The ritual reduced to the minimum was a hard boiled egg scooped out and filled with salt, or, in the Isle of Man, a salt herring, eaten skin, bones and all without speaking, could be used for divination in the same way. See Iona Opie and Moira Tatum, *A Dictionary of Superstition* (Oxford: Oxford University Press, 1989), p. 127.

52. Rowe (1796).
53. Reverend Stotherd Abdy, 'A Journal of a Visit into Berkshire' (1770) in A.A. Houblon, *The Houblon Family* (Constable, 1906), vol. 2.
54. G. Oliver, 'Old Christmas customs and popular superstitions of Lincolnshire', in *Gentleman's Magazine*, CII (1832), pp. 491–4.
55. Richard Sanders, *Physiognomie, Chiromencie, Metopscopie* (1653).
56. Reginald Scot, *The Discovery of Witchcraft* (1665) 3rd edition. One of Scot's cited cures for bewitched privities that will be of interest to historians of food were the instructions to eat 'a haggister or pie.'
57. Margaret Dods, *The Cook and Housewife's Manual* (Edinburgh, 1826).
58. Caird (1809).
59. May (1660).
60. Ann Peckham, *The Complete English Cook, or Prudent Housewife* (Leeds, 1767).
61. Peter Brears, 'Wassail! Celebrations in Hot Ale' in C. Anne Wilson (ed.), *Liquid Nourishment* (Edinburgh: Edinburgh University Press, 1993), pp. 125–133. See also Ivan Day (ed.), *Eat, Drink and be Merry. The British at Table 1600–2000* (Philip Wilson, 2000).
62. Manuscript receipt book *c.* 1660. Author's collection.
63. Anon., *The Art and Mystery of Vintners and Wine Coopers* (1682), p. 31.
64. Pierre Pomet, *A Compleat History of Druggs* (1725).
65. Herrick (1648).
66. Aubrey (1687).
67. Tobias Smollet, *The Expedition of Humphrey Clinker* (London, 1771). See also Charsley (1992), pp. 101–107.
68. William Carr, *The Dialect of Craven in the West Riding of the County of Yorkshire* (1828).
69. W. Henderson, *Notes on the Folk Lore of the Northern Counties of England and the Borders* (1866).
70. de Gaya (1748), p. 39.
71. de Gaya (1748), p. 40.

CHAPTER THREE

'SHE CAME FROM A GROANING VERY CHEERFUL...'[1] FOOD IN PREGNANCY, CHILDBIRTH AND CHRISTENING RITUAL

Layinka Swinburne and Laura Mason

Marriage was about property and getting heirs. In a patriarchal society, children, especially sons, were important. Any wedding was expected to be shortly followed by a birth, and a lying-in, usually of a month. During this time the child was baptized (enabling it to enter heaven, should it die) and the cycle ended with the churching of the mother.[2] Pregnancy and birth were uncertain, dangerous, and culturally lay within the undisclosed world of women, who celebrated their biological role with 'gossipings', all-female gatherings accompanied by plentiful food and drink. Baptism or christening (the terms are interchangeable) was essentially public, controlled by the male representatives of the church. In this essay, the covert world of pregnancy is examined first, and traditions to do with gossiping and christening celebrations considered second.

If, at times, the heirs turned up without a marriage taking place beforehand, some mothers at least must have had the benefit of advice and superstitions about what was considered best to eat. For the food historian, this is a difficult subject to research. Food and diet in pregnancy are generally represented by a few meagre, over-worked references to something which was so well known as to need no description. This indicates the gulf between written references and the wealth of oral traditions passed from woman to woman. Traces of this secrecy continue even now. Talk of 'eating for two', raspberry-leaf tea, and remnants of old celebrations or precautions remind us of former customs at what was known as 'the groaning time'. They are not quite submerged by officially promoted guidelines on healthy eating.

Overlaying this, gradual medicalization shifted emphasis from a natural process, to an 'interesting condition', to the invalidism of the nineteenth century. This affected dietary advice as different theories became current. In the twentieth century, new knowledge led to the understanding of diet in pregnancy as preparation for safe delivery and a healthy infant. Modern medicine has removed much of the danger to mother and child and, combined with social change, has disrupted the assumed link between weddings and births.

Historically, a reminder of the connection between marriage and child-bearing could even start at the wedding. In an ideal bridal feast of the fifteenth century, recorded as *Ffor to Serve a Lord*, guests were welcomed to the first course with a script borne by an *agnus dei* (a popular amulet for women in childbirth). After the company had worked their way through two courses of game, meat, and pies, the third was to be *viande royale*, a confection of quinces decorated with a cross of gold and silver leaf and lozenges of ginger and sugar plate.[3] Quinces were to beget wise children:

> There are worthy women, who during their pregnancy, eat a great deal of [quince] marmalade, which they say, is so that their children should be clever, having perhaps heard that it strengthens the retentive capacity of the brain.[4]

The culmination of the meal was most explicit: a cake decorated with a woman in child-bed and a script implying that children would soon follow. Nearer our time, in the Craven district of Yorkshire, the bride's pie 'was always made round with a very strong crust ornamented with various devices. In the middle of it was a fat laying hen, full of eggs,' perhaps also a representation of fecundity.[5]

Like all ideas about health and food in the early modern period, ideas about regimen and diet in pregnancy were influenced by Hippocratic theory. This was based on the four elements: earth, air, fire and water, and their properties of cold and heat, dryness and moisture. Every substance, including plants, foods and the four bodily humours, was classified according to its degrees of these properties. A person's character and appearance reflected the balance of the bodily humours, as summarized below:

Humour	*Character*	*Temperament*	*Organ*
Phlegm	cold and moist	phlegmatic	head
Blood	hot and moist	sanguine	heart
Black bile	hot and dry	melancholic	spleen
Yellow bile	cold and dry	choleric	liver

Food in Pregnancy, Childbirth and Christening Ritual

Figure 10. Tansy, an engraving from Culpeper. He said, 'Dame Venus was minded to pleasure women with child by this herb, for there grows not an herb fitter for their use than this.' It is not recommended that anyone follows this advice.

Each course of a banquet described in the same volume as the bridal feast in *Ffor to Serve a Lord* was decorated with a figure representing one of the temperaments: choleric, sanguine, melancholic and phlegmatic. Illness was manifested as an unfavourable change in the balance of the humours, and health could be restored by correcting this with foods and medicines having an opposite effect. Diet was a major part of the six non-naturals which should be taken into account in health matters – air and earth, food and drink, sleeping and waking, movement and rest, evacuation and retention, and the passions.[6]

Women and children were considered by nature to be cold and moist and prone to an excess of phlegm, so, from medieval times, they were advised to avoid cold, moist foods, especially raw fruits, salads and fish.[7] To adjust their temperaments, they needed to eat foods classified as moderately hot and dry, but the complexities of the system were such that it needed a doctor to work out the proper balance. If an imbalance in the humours was detected, it was advised that this should be corrected before pregnancy. Traditional beliefs and symbolism overlapped advice logically based on these theories.

Food in Pregnancy, Childbirth and Christening Ritual

The result of injury or external influences was to block the flow or cause excessive production overflowing to other parts of the body. 'Treatment' relied heavily on promoting the flow from whatever orifices were appropriate, and bleeding, both as a preventative and cure. Bleeding from the foot was resorted to, 'to bring on the courses'. Bleeding was recommended at two or three specified times during pregnancy but was otherwise dispensed with as potentially harmful.

Once married there were numerous hints on begetting children. Leek juice had a reputation, and many foods were thought to promote seed in both men and women: yolks of egg; fresh meat (especially of swine); cock sparrows; partridges; quails; boar's brains; and the testicles of animals such as boars, bulls and wolves; the marrow and fat of animals; pears; dates; almonds; figs; nuts; parsnip; turnip fried with honey and oil of beans; peas; and strong, sweet, full-bodied wine.[8] An Italian physician's recipe consisted of rabbit milk, pulverised snake skin and crayfish,[9] whilst if any more help was necessary, a 'Marmelate very comfortable and restorative for any Lord or Lady' contained eringo and saterion roots, nuts, cock stones [testicles], and other supposedly aphrodisiac ingredients, including cantarides [*sic*, Spanish fly].[10]

Amulets, charms, the advice of wise men and women might also be used, and the same could provide help in getting rid of an unwanted pregnancy.[11] In the mid-eighteenth century, *Aristotle's Masterpiece* advises: 'for barrenness let her take every day almond milk and goat's milk extracted with honey,' and use a pessary of fresh butter and oil of sweet almonds.[12] The border between food and medicine was vague and it is often hard to guess how a recipe was to be used.

When a woman became pregnant, she would certainly be bombarded with advice, but there is scant comment on diet in written sources (whose authors were mostly male). For many women, bearing virtually a child a year for many of their fertile years, pregnancy was almost their usual state. However, nothing was taken for granted as the pain and risks of childbirth were too often experienced.

In preventing abortion, food took its place beside magical aids, charms, prayers, an eagle-stone tied to the thigh, relics and holy girdles and other rituals to avoid witchcraft and ill-luck and ensure a safe delivery. Women had their own ways of promoting pregnancy and avoiding disaster. Protective rituals often involved tansy, so named from *athanasia* ('deathless'), and dedicated to the Virgin Mary (see opposite). It could be applied to the navel in a plaster or taken as a syrup either to prevent abortion or to promote labour.[13] An early work on midwifery, attributed to Trotula, a female physician associated with the School of Salerno, was the work used by Chaucer's physician. She advised elaborate changes in diet, herbal remedies, and medicated baths and pessaries to combat various gynaecological symptoms and advised for the mother-to-be: 'cause her to be cheerful. Give her refreshing food and get her used to bathing sometimes.'[14]

Food was also thought to influence the foetus, both in character and as a cause of birth marks. A woman with an excessive longing for a particular food could find her baby marked with the food, for example, a strawberry or a bunch of grapes, and it was debatable as to whether it was better to let her eat the food in moderation or to withhold it, as either too much or too little might increase the effect.

The whole process of gestation was mysterious, considered as a kind of cooking – the foetus was thought of as a cake in an oven.[15] In a French peasant custom a fresh loaf might be placed on the abdomen of a woman in labour to speed birth. There were fanciful ideas of the child being nourished by diverted menstrual blood, and the same blood was thought to be converted into milk once the child was born. This is illustrated in an extract from a medieval manuscript belonging to the monks of Bolton Abbey:

> From XXX daye ytt ys formyde in the forme of a mane…and froo the XL daye ytt begyns to be norcheyde w't' the bloode of the mothr by hys cowrs att the navylle…; and when that neyne monthes are fullfyllde, the blowde wherwythe that hee was norycheyde departs and assends uppe to the brests of the wooman, and ys theyre, as ytt wer, a thyke kreeme, and after hys byrthe hee ys norycheyde with mylke off his mothr.[16]

On the whole doctors left the matter of diet to women and their families and lay advisers, especially midwives. Culpeper, in his *Directory for Midwives* (1651),[17] had plenty of advice on diet as well as charms and herbal remedies for promoting conception and avoiding miscarriage. Dr George Cheyne strongly recommended a milk and vegetable diet to both men and women.[18] He also alluded to his friend, whom he called the milk doctor of Croydon. This man had brought many opulent families in his neighbourhood, who had continued some years after marriage without progeny, to have several fine children by keeping both parents for a considerable time on a diet of milk and vegetables.

Food in Pregnancy, Childbirth and Christening Ritual

Aristotle's Masterpiece gave advice on diet (including vestiges of the humoral theory) and lessons on anatomy and childbirth for both families and midwives:

> Let her observe a good diet suitable for her temperament, custom, condition, and quality. Let her put into her broth those herbs that purify it as sorrel, lettuce, succory and burrage for they will purge and purify the blood.

And:

> If she desires fish let it be fresh and such as is taken out of rivers and running streams. Let her eat quinces of marmalade to strengthen her child, sweet almonds, honey and full ripe grapes are also good.[19]

The book also instructed on foods and herbs appropriate to each month but acknowledged that because of 'loathings and longings' it might be difficult to prescribe an exact diet. In a later edition of the work one maxim was: 'a women after conception ought to be looked upon as indisposed or sick even though in good health.'[20] This was taken to heart by many women, but more sensible doctors railed against females who confined themselves to the house and lived on caudles and slops to the detriment of their health.

Gradual medicalization of birth in the eighteenth and nineteenth centuries stimulated some interest in diet but, unfortunately, at the same time pregnancy was also transformed from a natural to an 'interesting' state, and finally to an 'abnormal' one.

William Buchan made a distinction between poor and wealthier women, to the detriment of the latter, in his popular work *Domestic Medicine* of 1796:

> Mothers who do not eat a sufficient quantity of solid food, not enjoy the benefit of free air and exercise, can neither have wholesome juices themselves, nor afford proper nourishment to an infant.

Such habits were

> a strong proof of the bad taste and wrong education of modern females....A delicate female brought up indoors an utter stranger to exercise and open air who lives on tea and other slops may bring an infant into the world but it will be hardly fit to live.[21]

No doubt this made work for others in the health field, like the Smedleys,

Food in Pregnancy, Childbirth and Christening Ritual

who ran a fashionable hydrotherapy establishment at Matlock in the mid-eighteenth century. Diet was as much part of the regime as the baths, and *Mrs Smedley's Ladies' Manual of Practical Hydropathy* went into dozens of editions. The advice covered both pregnancy and lying-in:

> a great deal depends, during the whole of pregnancy, on the person taking great care in diet and taking water as the only liquid and brown bread, vegetables, farinaceous puddings and milk for the principal food. Better with little or no flesh meat.[22]

Even in the twentieth century, some odd theories prevailed over common sense. A Bradford gynaecologist, Andreas Rabagliati, had specially weird ideas and preached against over-eating. He calculated the increase in weight of the baby and placenta and, from this, concluded that a pregnant woman need not eat more than two ounces of food a day extra and, worse still, should avoid protein. Children, he thought, needed no more than two meals a day.

Another enthusiast, M.L. Holbrook, recommended a diet low in minerals in his book *Parturition without Pain*,[23] omitting bread and other foods rich in minerals like calcium, in the belief that the phosphate in wheat would make the baby's head harder and make parturition painful. He advised vegetables to dissolve any bone-making material so that the bones of the unborn child would remain gristly. Rabagliati quoted an Australian doctor who claimed that 'fruit babies' thrived better and had better bones and teeth than the 'bread and meat babies' in an experiment.[24]

The Vitalogists commented that:

> [the] fecundity of the human race is diminished by the indolent and luxurious mode of life prevalent among the rich, while it is augmented by the industrious habits and spare diet of the poor…Spices, spiced meat, sausage and all highly seasoned food and late suppers must be refrained from. Plainly cooked animal food once a day, well boiled vegetables, ripe fruits, … rice, tapioca, [and] arrow root will rarely disagree with the stomach. Just about everything else must be rejected.[25]

In modern times, scientific study of nutritional needs and the discovery of vitamins and other essential substances have been the foundation of better advice. It took a great step forward in the Second World War and is founded on positive encouragement of good and varied eating, with supplements of

Food in Pregnancy, Childbirth and Christening Ritual

essential foods like milk and orange juice, rather than restrictions based on false theories.

The actual time of childbirth was known variously as confinement, lying-in or, more vividly, the 'groaning time'. At this time, the midwife was the mainstay for most women. An early work on obstetrics advised that birth might be speeded up by giving a woman the urine of the man whose child she bears to drink, bitch's urine, or the milk of another woman.[26] Culpeper offered gromwell seed in woman's milk to the same end.[27] Dr Chamberlain opined that the woman's milk might be repugnant. Pleasanter things were usually on offer. *Aristotle's Masterpiece* suggested that 'if her travail be tedious she may take chicken or mutton broth or a poached egg.' Tansy, applied to the navel or given as a syrup, was also popular with midwives. Perhaps because of its bitterness, the *etrog*, or citron, was used in much the same way by Jewish women[28] to promote labour and prevent miscarriage.

Three of the four remedies connected with childbirth in Mrs Eden's Receipt Book (Ripley Castle, 1694) contained saffron. A syrup recipe, requiring half a pound of saffron steeped in a quart of sack, was recorded almost a century later (*c.* 1778) in a Knaresborough Receipt Book[29] (see recipes, p. 151). Saffron syrup had many other uses but was mentioned by Fernie as specially associated with childbirth.[30] The amount of saffron cited must have meant the recipe was expensive to make. In a syrup, saffron was considered to have the virtue of strengthening the heart, although it was used in other confections: for instance, in Lancashire it was an essential ingredient of cakes or biscuits (and is still used in cakes in the south west).

Midwives gained a reputation for drunkenness, satirized by Charles Dickens in the character of Mrs Gamp. This was probably undeserved, but drink was available for all attending the birth. It was not unknown for mothers to join in. Dr Giffard (1734) complained that:

> what in some measure occasioned the difficulty, was the woman being stupefied and senseless from the quantity of strong liquors that was given her, and her smoking Tobacco, so that she was very drunk and no ways capable of pursuing directions, nor of assisting me by bearing down at the time of my extracting the child.[31]

However, some recipes considered suitable for women in labour were not innocent, even in the nineteenth century. Maria Rundell's recipe for a Caudle for the Sick and Lying-in[32] began mildly enough with oatmeal, water and allspice, but finished with beer and a glass of gin (see recipes, p. 151). Buchan declared that pregnancy was not a disease, but banned cordials and condemned the woman to near starvation on water-gruel during labour. He grudgingly allowed that, 'those whose spirits cannot be supported without solid food and generous liquors – to such a glass of wine and a bit of chicken must be allowed.' In the mid-nineteenth century the Smedley regime was relatively harsh – gruel the first day, then Scotch oatmeal porridge, beef tea, weak black tea and bread and butter, stewed pears and ripe grapes. However, the Vitalogists announced that in lying-in there was no need for slops and restrictions:

> We allow a mutton chop for dinner on the first day, for the other meals well made oatmeal porridge, cold-buttered toast or bread and butter, a cupful of arrowroot or gruel and light farinaceous puddings.[33]

Herbs and foods were chosen to promote the flow of milk in the mother or a wet-nurse. The family were warned to watch her diet:

> I prescribe white bread, good meat, rice and lettuce, peas, beans, almonds and hazelnuts, pure wine, peas, beans, and milk gruel, if the milk gives out. She should avoid onions, garlic, sour food, over-salted food and vinegar.[34]

Culpeper recommended fennel, milk thistle and lettuce, whilst Eliza Smith favoured lentil posset.[35] However, the baby's first food was not always what one might expect. Beliefs about breast-milk and colostrum sometimes led to the baby being starved for twenty-four hours or fed on strange mixtures of butter or a piece of meat, to stave off the mother's longings or ward off the evil eye and witchcraft. In *Good Things in England* (1932) Florence White said of rum butter in the Lake District that, 'a small piece is put in the baby's mouth as its first taste of earthly food.'[36] Honey and wine were sometimes given. Buchan pointed out that:

> almost every person is struck with the idea of their being weak. Accordingly wines are universally mixed with the first foods of children. This naturally suggests the need of cordials.[37]

Daffey's elixir and Godfrey's cordial were both beloved of midwives. The powerful sedative effect of the laudanum and alcohol in these sent many an infant to its grave. Paps, most often of boiled bread and milk or later of arrowroot and other farinaceous mixtures, were sometimes given, in one case

Food in Pregnancy, Childbirth and Christening Ritual

at the insistence of a seventeenth-century husband who did not want his infant fed by 'some pocky nurse.'[38] Royalty set the fashion for or against breast-feeding in different periods.

The fate of the placenta and caul was another focus of rituals which might involve their careful disposal or preservation for magical and medicinal purposes. The placenta might also be eaten, either raw or cooked, a practice which is sometimes reported, with raised eyebrows, even in the late twentieth century. A seventeenth-century recipe for the falling sickness (epilepsy) advises powdered, dried placenta to be taken in ale or beer every morning for six days as an infallible cure.[39] Powdered placenta could also be used as a remedy to speed up the birth.[40]

Whilst the expectant mother was getting on with delivery, there was the prospect of a celebration for the community. The whole family was involved in preparations, and its support was essential. The dowager Countess of Westmorland came to London especially for the lying-in of her daughter, Lady Anne Clifford (although she missed the crucial moment: whilst researching family documents in the Tower she was locked in by unexpectedly early closing of gates). The men had their own priorities: 'I brewed my groaning beer,' recorded Samuel Sewall, in 1678.[41]

In the sixteenth and seventeenth centuries, female friends and relatives were known collectively as 'gossips', originally God-sibs or 'siblings in God'. The gossips were originally there not just to assist, but to witness the birth, preventing deception or substitution of another baby, and act as sponsors at its baptism. Older women were the mainstay. In *A Midsummer Night's Dream*, Puck sang an uncomplimentary song which also records two of the ingredients, ale and roast crab apples:

> And sometime lurk I in a gossip's bowl
> In the very likeness of a roasted crab;
> And when she drinks against her lips I bob
> And on her withered dewlap pour the ale.[42]

Some brought young children with them, but pregnant women were not allowed, although there were superstitions that women wishing to become pregnant would soon follow the example set by sympathetic influence. They all provided support for the 'woman in the straw'. As well as ale, groaning-cakes were shared by the gossips. John Aubrey commented:

Food in Pregnancy, Childbirth and Christening Ritual

At Wendlebury, and other places, they [the women] bring their cakes at a gossiping, and give a large cake to the father of the child which they call a rocking-cake.[43]

In Northern England, the groaning-cake brought by one of the family friends came to be an important symbol.[44] A large cheese was also essential. In some places the cake was to be set on top of the cheese. The groaning-cake or cheese was to be cut by the doctor or midwife into the exact number of pieces as those present as otherwise bad luck would follow. Ability to confer fertility or good luck on the possessor might also be attributed to the groaning-cake, to which end a piece (usually the first) could be retained by an unmarried or childless visitor and hidden under the pillow to ensure fertility. The cake could be a spice or pepper cake (see recipes, p. 152) or a rich plum cake; in East Yorkshire it was often a spiced rye loaf. Provided all went well, the groaning was a time of celebration and would be followed by the christening and churching. If not, the same cakes and cheeses would no doubt serve for the funeral of mother, babe or both. In another ritual (at its christening), the child was said to be passed through a hole left by cutting the groaning cheese from the centre, as some people still cut a Stilton.[45]

Generally, the mother might be considered in need of reviving with flasks of cordials, bowls of caudle or broth and cups of posset. The preferred drink for the new mother was a caudle, and wine. Cordials might be given too, but although long regarded as having medicinal and strengthening properties, eighteenth-century doctors condemned them as too stimulating.[46] In a satire, a husband complained of the expense of finding money for the midwife, and also for her nurse:

> who must make for her warme broaths and costly caudles enough for both herself and her mistresse, being of a mind to fare no worse than she; if her mistresse be fedde with partridge, plover, woodcocks, quailes, or any such like, the nurse must be partaker with her in all these dainties.[47]

It was also common to give money to the mother, servants, the midwife and nurse.[48] In 1706 Richard Kaye wrote in his diary, 'Gave Deborah the mid-wife 5s … John Leigh brought my wife a Groaning-cake, gave her 6d. My wife gave John Kaye's wife in child-bed 2s 6d and syrup of ginger.'[49]

Distribution of groaning-cake echoes more elaborate, high-status celebrations associated with births recorded in several European countries. It is

Food in Pregnancy, Childbirth and Christening Ritual

probable that these rituals developed among wealthy families in Renaissance Italy and spread to the rest of Europe. They can first be seen in Italian paintings of the birth of the Virgin or Saint Anne, showing the *brigate* – female friends and relatives – gathered round in their finery. In one such painting, a women in the procession carried the glorious, highly decorated *desco da parto* [birth-tray], covered with a black-work embroidered cloth, which would bear both symbolic and traditional foods and emphasize the ceremony of childbirth.

Despite the large number of surviving trays and depictions of birth scenes, the offerings remain a matter of conjecture. The importance of salt in the ritual is shown by the separate *saliera* or salt-pot included in majolica sets of later birth-ware.[50] Flasks of cordials and sweetened wines are always present. Other items probably included caudles, almond dishes such as *bianco mangiare*, sweetmeats of many kinds, sugared pine nuts and preserved fruits. A later Dutch birth scene shows a tray of sweetmeats being handed round.

Early references to the use of sweetmeats at English birth celebrations come from Holinshed's descriptions of the births of Henry VIII's children. His first child by Catherine of Aragon in 1510 (a boy, christened Henry, who died at about seven weeks old) had a splendid baptism followed by numerous masques, pageants and 'bankets' (banquets).[51] Elizabeth, born in 1533 to Anne Boleyn, so disappointed her father by being female that he did not attend the christening, but Holinshed tells that afterwards, 'Then was brought in wafers, comfets, and ipocrasse in such plentie, that eurie man had as much as he would desire'.[52] In 1537, another boy (later King Edward VI) was borne to Henry's third queen, Jane Seymour. John Strype, writing about the reformation of the Church of England, described the prince's christening at Hampton Court. The chapel was hung with tapestries, the way thickly strewn with rushes, and the font was of silver and gilt. In procession, esquires, knights and gentlemen walked in pairs carrying torches, which were not lit until after the christening. Spices, wafers and wine were served:

> For the serving the Lady Mary and the Lady Elizabeth with spices, wafers and wine, the Lord Hastings bore the cup to the Lady Mary, and the Lord Delaware another cup to Lady Elizabeth. The Lord Dacre of the South bare the spice-plates to them both, the Lord Cobham the wafers, and the Lord Montague uncovered the spice-plates. The Bishop that administered was served with spice, wine and wafers, by three of

Food in Pregnancy, Childbirth and Christening Ritual

the ancient knights appointed by the Lord Chamberlain. The Archbishop of Canterbury, the Duke of Norfolk, godfathers at the font, and the Duke of Suffolk, godfather at the confirmation, were served with like spices, wafers and wine, by three knights, also by the Lord Chamberlain appointed. All other estates and gentlemen within the Church and Court were served with spice and hippocrass; and all others with bread and sweet wine.[53]

'Spices' – sugar-coated, spiced comfits, such as aniseed and caraway, were generally considered medicinal, especially as aids to digestion. They were also indicators of status and wealth, and their connection with ideas about luck and increase seems to go back a long way.

An association between sweetmeats and christenings is well documented in England in the seventeenth century. A list of foods from the 1617 steward's account of the Shuttleworth family of Gawthorpe in West Yorkshire shows what might have been expected:[54]

Bought of Mr Leaver the 12th Sept 1617. – A Note of the spices at the tyme of my Mistress lyinge in child bedd

Almand comfetts	3lb	4s
Oaliander comfetts	3lb	4s
Annelseed do	2lb	2s 8d
Sjnimon do	1lb	1s 6d
Ginger do	1lb	1s 6d
Orrideye do	1lb	1s 6d
Rose do	1lb	1s 6d
Vyolett do	1lb	1s 6d
Rosemary do	1lb	1s 6d
Ambergrice do	1lb	6s 6d
Muskedines	½lb	3s
Marchpaine stuffe	2lb	4s
Macoro wines	1lb	2s
Naples biskett	1lb	2s
Dryed suckett	2lb	5s
Fyne past of plumes	3lb	12s
Candel spices	2lb	12s
Quinces plate	2lb	8s

Food in Pregnancy, Childbirth and Christening Ritual

Damsones pl.	1lb	3s 4d
Cheries pl.	1lb	4s
Barberies pl.	1lb	4s
Raspberries pl.	1lb	4s
Goosberies pl.	1lb	4s
Peare plumes	1lb	4s
For 7 pouts		4s
For a box		1s 2d
For a porter carrying them to Islington		2s 6d
Summa		£5 2s 4d

Bought from a London confectioner and spicer, this represents a huge outlay. (In contrast, the Shuttleworths handed out only 3s 8d to Widow Sonckie, 'for soe much ale and breade in the tyme of her child bedd,' the same year.) The items above suggest that the family offered comfits of many sorts, preserved fruits and sweet biscuits to visitors. Incidentally, an opportunistic writer suggested that the midwife could use a sugared almond in the anus to cure a constipated new-born baby.

Visitors and those attending christenings expected to take home a few sweetmeats. Brand, in his *Antiquities*, stated:

> It appears to have been anciently the custom, at Christening entertainments, for the guests not only to eat as much as they pleased, but also, for the ladies at least, to carry away as much as they liked in their pockets.[55]

He followed this with a quotation from the *Batchelar's Banquet*, which was outspoken about the custom:

> what cost and trouble it will be…to have all things fine against the Christening day, what store of Sugar, Biskets, Comphets and Carowayes, Marmilade, and martchpaine, with all kinds of sweete suckets, and superfluous banqueting stuffe, with a hundred other odde and needlesse trifles, which at that time must fill the pockets of daintie dames[56]

Poor Robin's *Almanack* of 1676, too, makes an explicit connection between sweets and christenings:

> For the nurse, the child to dandle,
> Sugar, sope, spic'd pots and candle,
> A groaning chair, and eke a cradle,

Food in Pregnancy, Childbirth and Christening Ritual

Blanckets of several scantling,
Therin for to wrap the bantling,
Sweetmeats from comfit-makers trade,
When the child's a christian made.[57]

Pepys recorded several christenings in his diaries, including one on 10 July 1664, at which there was a good service of sweetmeats. In view of this, it is surprising to discover that the French traveller Henri Misson, whose memoirs of his visit to England were first published in 1698, remarked that the English custom was not to make great feasts at the birth of a child but, 'they drink a glass of wine and eat a bit of a certain cake, which is seldom made but upon these occasions.'[58]

When the use of comfits at rites of passage generally died out in Britain is unclear. It remains widespread on the Continent, where sugared almonds, packed in lace or net, are given to guests at christenings (and weddings). A related custom also exists in Holland: visitors to a house after a birth are offered buttered rusks scattered with *musjies* (literally, 'little mice' – pink and white sugared aniseed), recalling the seventeenth-century festive marchpane stuck with comfits. Different countries preserve different aspects of customs.

It is cake which remained the constant in British – or at least English – childbirth celebrations, expected at groanings and christenings. In Shakespeare's *Famous History of the Life of King Henry VIII* (1612), 'a Porter and his Man' are attempting to restore order amongst a mass of people who have broken into the palace yard whilst Elizabeth's christening is taking place. The porter tells them to go, saying, 'you must be seeing christenings? do you look for ale and cakes here you rude rascals?'[59]

In 1664, Samuel Pepys recorded on the 17 July:

After dinner walked to my Lord's [Lord Sandwich] – and there found him and much other guests at table at dinner, and it seems they have christened his young son today, called him James; I got a piece of cake.

On 18 October 1666, he stood godfather for a child of a friend; after the ceremony:

the poor people of the house had good wine and good cake: and she [Mrs Lovett] a pretty woman in her lying-in dress. It cost me near 40s the whole christening: to midwife, 20s – nurse, 10s – maid, 2s 6d and the coach 5s – I was very well satisfied with what I have done.

Food in Pregnancy, Childbirth and Christening Ritual

John Aubrey observed that, 'At Burcester, in Oxfordshire, at a christening, the women bring everyone a cake, and present one first to the minister, if present.'[60] Brand related a custom which seems to have involved a kind of ritual exchange, in which the midwife provided a slice of bread and a slice of cheese, 'which are presented to the first person they meet in the procession to church at a christening.' In return, this person had to wish the child three different things, in addition to health and beauty.

Shakespeare's reference shows that cake had already become one of the foods expected at a christening. It presumably followed the general development of English fruit cakes, from something resembling lightly sweetened bread, through a gradual process of sweetening and enrichment, to become the modern rich fruit cake. The first specific recipe for a christening-cake so far located is 'Cake made for Peggy Lovet's Christening, May 15th, 1744', quoted by Florence White in *Good Things in England*.[61] This was a yeasted fruit cake with lots of currants, peel and brandy, similar to eighteenth-century bride-cake recipes (see recipes, p. 152). By 1861, Mrs Beeton gave a single recipe, for 'rich bride or christening cake'.[62] This was echoed in *Cassell's Universal Cookbook* (1901)[63] in which the reader is referred from 'christening cake' to the bride-cake recipe.

Records remain silent about decorations for early cakes but it is probable that ornaments appropriate to the theme of babies were used. There are two moulds for figures of babies in swaddling clothes in the Pinto Collection,[64] but they are unprovenanced. The 1901 edition of the *Book of Household Management* illustrates a model of a cradle for the top of such a cake,[65] and late twentieth-century practice includes sugar or icing models of cradles and babies. The origin of the contemporary idea of keeping the top tier of a wedding-cake for the subsequent christening is unknown, but it is unlikely to have originated until the late nineteenth century. Before this, wedding-cakes mostly seem to have had only one tier.

Details of other foods used at formal christening celebrations are sparse. Pepys does not say what else Lord Sandwich and his guests were having for dinner. One food which records indicate was used in the nineteenth and twentieth centuries is a chine, which, as 'stuffed chine', is remembered as a feature of christenings in Lincolnshire to the present day.[66] This consists of the section of backbone and meat from between the shoulder blades of a bacon hog, preserved by salting. When required for cooking, the meat is slashed vertically on either side of the bone and the slashes stuffed with immense quantities of chopped parsley: 'a small bathful,' was quoted by Jane Grigson.[67] The meat is tied in a cloth and simmered in water, pressed and cooled. Carved lengthways, parallel to the bone, it presents a spectacular contrast of colours: stripes of pink, brined lean and white fat, crossed at right angles by dark green streaks of herbs. Grigson records that the French writer Verlaine noted chine as a dish peculiar to Lincolnshire when he spent a year there as a schoolmaster in the mid-1870s, and that he searched for it in vain in other parts of the country. However, it was known. Florence White notes:

> At Aldsworth, Northleach, Gloucestershire, they had a favourite dish for the sowing feast which was usually held on the last Sunday in April. It consisted of a good big fore-chine, sometimes called the 'christening chine' with large suet puddings. Mrs Caudle, of Honeybourne, who was the daughter of a Herefordshire farmer, says 'The christening or fore-chine was cut down each side of the backbone or chine of a pig and it was so called because one was generally saved for a christening.' Miss Lanchbury of West Kissington, Gloucestershire, says her mother always cooked a christening chine for 'Mothering Sunday'.[68]

Chine also appears in Joseph Wright's *Dialect Dictionary* (1898), with citations from West Yorkshire, Lincolnshire, Worcestershire, Shropshire, Wiltshire and west Somerset. The quote from Shropshire is enlightening: 'Cut a good chine, as the offil lasses us most the 'ear; the flitches an' the 'ams be wantin for rent an' other things.'[69] A judicious and generous hand could cut the family pig so that a part which was counted amongst the offal – and therefore not sold to provide income – was a substantial and meaty joint, preserved by salting and available for unpredictable events, such as christenings. Chines could be cut from other meat animals: beef, mutton, veal, venison and pork are recorded in seventeenth- and eighteenth-century cookery books, in elaborate recipes with stuffings and sauces of herbs.

These records relating to chine also cast interesting light on further dialogue in Shakespeare's *Life of Henry VIII*, where 'the Man' declares:

> …if I spared any
> That had a head to hit, either young or old,
> He or she, cuckold or cuckold maker,
> Let me ne'er hope to see a chine again.

Food in Pregnancy, Childbirth and Christening Ritual

This statement about a chine has been interpreted variously as meaning to eat meat, or as the man being fed up with the back views of the crowd. It is impossible to know if it was also a pun on a cut of meat, but worth noting that, by the nineteenth century, the latter was deeply embedded in folk practices at christenings.

Customs observed by the poor are difficult to trace at any time. In 1647, Mother Bumbey had prepared 'an hogshead of nappy ale, with a gammon of bacon and other good accoutrements' to entertain witnesses and gossips after a baptism.[70] In *Traditional Food in Yorkshire* Peter Brears included a short section on foods associated with 'Headwashings', as baptisms were termed in some northern dialects. He quotes a 'yed-weshin' tea from Saddleworth, which echoed the gossips' gathering; the guests – female friends and relations of the mother:

> sat down to rum and tea, beef and bread, oven bottom muffins, crumpets, seed bread, thodden cake, threddle cake, shouting Roger currant bread, about ten currants in a loaf, and home-made blackberry jam. As soon as the tea was over and the old fashioned china sided away into the corner cupboard, [they] set on the table a bottle of elderberry wine for the spinsters and a bottle of rhubarb wine for the wed women. The guests then gathered round the evening fire, and some lit their pipes.[71]

By the late eighteenth century, amongst the gentry, food at christening celebrations seems to have been entirely a matter of individual choice. On 28 January 1780, after christening a child of his friends the Custances, Reverend Woodforde was invited to a dinner:

> a Calf's Head, boiled Fowl and Tongue, a Saddle of Mutton rosted on the Side Table, and a fine Swan rosted with Currant Jelly Sauce for the first Course. The Second Course a couple of Wild Fowl called Dun Fowls [probably pochard], Larks, Blanmange, Tarts etc. etc. and a good Desert of Fruit after amongst which was a Damson Cheese. I never eat a bit of Swan before, and I think it good eating with sweet sauce. The Swan was killed 3 weeks before it was eat and yet not had the lest bad taste in it.

On 26 June 1792, after christening another of the Custances' children:

> We dined and spent the Afternoon at Weston House. ... Dinner boiled Tench, Peas Soup, a Couple of boiled Chicken and Pig's Face, hashed

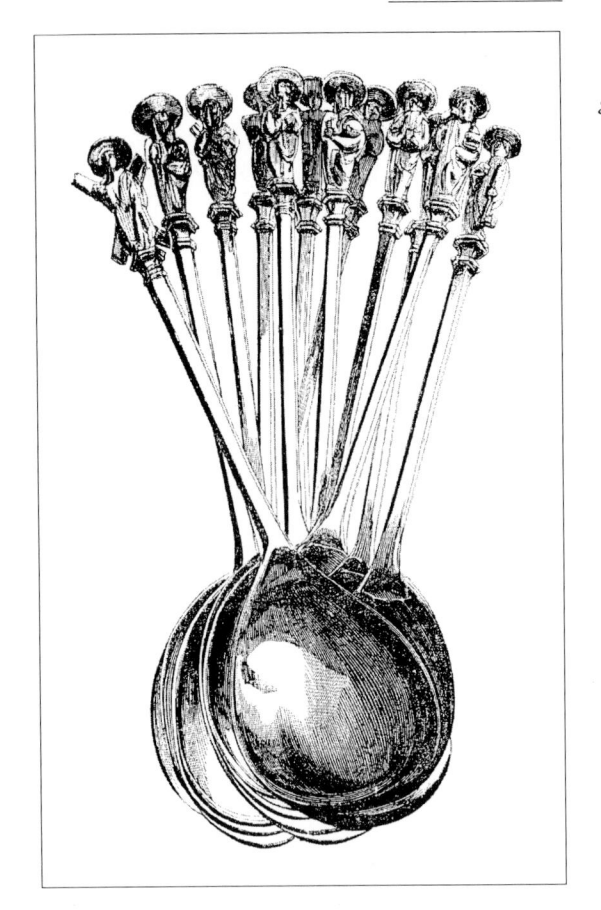

Food in Pregnancy, Childbirth and Christening Ritual

Figure 11. Apostle spoons, a traditional gift from godparent to godchild. From William Hone, The Every-day Book, *1838.*

Calf's Head, Beans and rosted Rump of Beef with New Potatoes &c. 2nd course rosted Duck and green Peas, a very fine Leveret rosted, Strawberry Cream, Jelly, Puddings &c. Desert – Strawberries, Cherries and last Years nonpareils. About 7 o'clock after Coffee and Tea we got to Cards.[72]

These meals were generous in scale, but not unusual in either size or composition for the late eighteenth century.

There is little obvious information about the composition of christening meals in the nineteenth century. One problem is that novels – a rich source of material about food habits for this time – rarely involve christenings, except to make a moral point, such as the unfortunate Tess of the D'Urbevilles who baptized her illegitimate child herself. Charles Dickens introduced a christening into *Dombey and Son* which involved, 'a cold collation, set forth in cold pomp of glass and silver, and looking more like a dead dinner lying in state than a social refreshment.'[73] The food included a cold fillet of veal, a cold preparation of calf's head, cold fowls, ham, patties and salad, with champagne and sherry to drink. This appears to be a case of using food to create atmosphere, rather than an exact reflection of early Victorian habits relating to christenings. Dickens did, however, make the godparents in his story give entirely traditional gifts: a knife, fork and spoon in a case, and a mug.

Appointment of sponsors or godparents to provide moral guidance and other help to the child was an important aspect of christening. Godparents were an official extension of the 'gossip'. They were expected to present gifts at baptism; often these were objects of tableware. Royal births required splendid gifts: godparents for the Princess Elizabeth in 1533 were the Archbishop of Canterbury (Cranmer), who gave a standing cup of gold; the Duchess of Norfolk, who gave three gilt bowls, and the Marchioness of Exeter, whose gift was three engraved gilt standing bowls. Gifts for Prince Edward in 1537 included: 'three great bowls and two great pots of silver and gilt', given by the Archbishop, and 'two great flagons and two great pots of silver and gilt', given by the Duke of Suffolk.[74]

Gifts from godparents to children in less exalted situations were silver spoons or drinking vessels. As well as being valuable in themselves, these can be seen as statements of intent towards socializing the child into good table manners. A silver mug, spoon or nursery set of knife, fork and spoon is sometimes still presented to a baby. Even in the nineteenth century, eating implements, such as knives, spoons, and drinking vessels, were often carried as personal possessions. This made such gifts even more significant. They were the first step in fitting the child up to be a functioning member of society.

Other, more symbolic, gifts to the baby in northern England included an egg, salt and a piece of silver so that the child might never know want or hunger and to ward off the evil eye.[75] In some places salt was to be hidden in the cradle, which might also be decorated with rowan sprigs to ward off witchcraft.[76] Salt was also used in the Roman Catholic baptism ceremony to signify the spiritual salt, the word of God.[77]

Returning to the drinks, 'wetting the baby's head' has become a colloquial phrase for a party in honour of a new-born, but it also obliquely indicates the sacrament of baptism in which water is poured over the baby's head as part of a church service. A persistent emphasis on liquids, especially alcoholic, runs though birth and christening celebrations. On occasions of national

Food in Pregnancy, Childbirth and Christening Ritual

importance, the community in the widest sense was invited to partake, as for the first-born to Henry and Catherine in 1510. Holinshed, writing about seventy years later, says:

> on New Yeares daie the first daie of Januarie the queene was delivered of a prince to the great gladnesse of the realme, for the honour of whome fiers were made and diuerse vessels with white wine set for such as would take thereof in certaine streets in London.[78]

Strype mentions a christening of 1562 which was concluded with a great banquet, consisting of wafers and hypocras: 'French, Gascoign and Rhenish wines with great plenty.'[79]

Drink and the baby could be explicitly linked, as in Dent on the north-western edge of Yorkshire, where 'the shout' or 'crying out' brought neighbouring women to the birth:

> as soon as the baby had made its first wail, the nearest neighbour immediately ran from house to house to spread the good news, all the womenfolk then picking up their warming pans and rushing to the house to celebrate with a feast of a particular kind of bread, rum butter and home-made wines. While the women were thus employed, the father and his male friends proceeded to wash the baby's head with brandy before enjoying numerous glasses of strong drink.[80]

Further to the north-west, in the Lake District, rum butter was a traditional offering for those who called to see a mother and her new child. Florence White commented that, 'Rum butter is sometimes called "sweet butter"; a bowl of it is always prepared before the coming of a baby; it is offered to visitors.'[81]

The clergy were not exempt from heavy drinking. In eighteenth-century Anglesey, Lewis Morris recorded:

> In Christenings when the christening is over then the father invites home his friends & ye Parson to drink ye health of ye woman in ye straw, and after dinner this they do for ye first part so plentifully till they can drinck no more for that day, money to ye midwife, to ye nurse and to the maid. Home stark drunk.[82]

And in 1801, in Norfolk, Reverend Woodforde noted that:

Food in Pregnancy, Childbirth and Christening Ritual

Mr Maynard [his curate] dined & spent the Afternoon with us. Mrs Custance and Lady Bacon met him as they came near my House and he appeared to them disguised in Liquor; which I heard afterwards was the Case – he having been to Mr Mann's to name a Child, they perhaps urging him to drink. ... Mr Maynard left us about 7 this Evening and perfectly sober and well. I would not by no means push the Glass on fast as I was uneasy about his drinking too much this Morn' at Manns he having been there to name Mann's Child.[83]

Cressy cites numerous other records of clergymen joining carousing gossips and male guests at baptism celebrations.[84] Finally, about a month after the birth, the cycle begun by recognition of a pregnancy was completed by the ceremony of 'churching' the mother. Interpretations of the significance and meaning of this ceremony vary, but it seems that this, too, was often seen as an opportunity for celebration.

In modern times, medical supervision during pregnancy and the fashion for having the father present at delivery have eroded the gender-specific aspects of childbirth celebrations. Whilst the father is often still treated to an informal drinking party, the gossips' gathering, with its overtones of female bonding, has disappeared. Parties associated with christenings have become the least obvious of the three major rites of passage. In higher status celebrations, the formal baptism is followed by a decorous lunch or afternoon tea party for close family, godparents and friends. The distinguishing feature is the presence of the cake and champagne, which now carries the burden of a formerly much more extensive and public celebration that acknowledged childbirth as the culmination of a commonplace, natural and expected process, rather than as isolated events in the long lives of individual mothers.

Food in Pregnancy, Childbirth and Christening Ritual

Notes

1. Cited in *O.E.D.* art. 'groaning', quoting Samuel Sewall, *Diary*, 16 Feb. 1682.
2. A ceremony which is not examined here, although there are indications that it was celebrated with special feasts. See David Cressy, *Birth, Marriage and Death: ritual, religion, and the life-cycle in Tudor and Stuart England* (Oxford: Oxford University Press, 1997).
3. Frederick J. Furnivall, *Early English Meals and Manners* (Early English Text Society Original Series 32, 1868, reprinted 1931), p. 359.
4. Jacques Gélis *A History of Childbirth* (Cambridge: Polity Press, 1991), p. 88, quoting Primerose, *Erreurs Vulgaires*.
5. William Carr, *The Dialect of Craven* 51, cited in Peter Brears, *Traditional Food in Yorkshire* (Edinburgh: John Donald Ltd, 1987), p. 186.
6. Carole Rawcliffe, *Medicine and Society in Later Medieval England* (Gloucester: Alan Sutton Publishing Ltd., 1994), p. 37.
7. Andrew Boord, *A Compendious Regiment or A Dyetary of Helthe* (1542), ed. F.J. Furnivall (Early English Text Society, e.s. 10, 1870).
8. Beryl Rowland, *Medieval Woman's Guide to Health* (Croom Helm, 1981), p. 198.
9. Jacqueline M. Musacchio, *The Art and Rituals of Childbirth in Renaissance Italy* (Yale University Press, 1999), p. 140.
10. Anon., *A Closet for Ladies and Gentlewomen* (1608), p. 44.
11. Keith Thomas, *Religion and the Decline of Magic* (1971, reprinted Penguin Books, 1993), p. 222.
12. *Aristotle's Masterpiece, c.* 1755. The origins of this popular work are obscure, but it was probably very influential, as it was reprinted numerous times from the late seventeenth century onwards.
13. W.T. Fernie, *Herbal Simples* (Bristol: John Wright and Co, 1914), p. 507.
14. Rowland (1981), p. 95.
15. Gélis (1991), p. 65.
16. T.D. Whitaker *The History and Antiquities of the Deanery of Craven in the County of York* (1878) 3rd edition, vol. II.
17. Nicholas Culpeper, *A Directory for Midwives: Or, A Guide for Women, in their Conception, Bearing and Suckling their Children* (1651).
18. H.T. Ruddock, *Vitalogy* (Chicago: Vitalogy Association, 1926), p. 414, quoting Dr George Cheyne. The reference does not say which of his works, but it is probably *The English Malady* (1733) in which he wrote at length of the benefits of a milk and vegetable diet.
19. *Aristotle's Masterpiece* (1840), p. 95.
20. *Aristotle's Masterpiece* (1840), p. 94.
21. W. Buchan, *Domestic Medicine* (1796), p. 2.
22. Caroline Anne Smedley, *Mrs Smedley's Ladies' Manual of Practical Hydropathy* (James, Blackwood and Co, 1758) 14th edition, p. 30.
23. M.L. Holbrook, *Parturition Without Pain* (New York: Wood and Holbrook, 1877), quoted in *Vitalogy*, p. 358.
24. Andreas Rabagliati, *Conversations with Women* (1909), p. 226.
25. Ruddock (1926), p. 353.
26. Quoted in Audrey Eccles, *Obstetrics and Gynaecology in Tudor and Stuart England* (Kent State University Press, 1982), p. 102.
27. Nicholas Culpeper, *The Complete Herbal or English Physician* (1826, reprint Manchester, 1981), p. 65. 'Gromwell' indicates plants of the genus *Lithospermum*.
28. Gillian Riley, *A Feast for the Eyes* (Yale University Press, 1997), p. 10. The paradox of apparently opposite effects of the same agent is one of the glories of humoral theory.

Promoting well-being and proper action of the uterus meant correcting the balance of humours and flow of vital spirits, thus enhancing whatever it was supposed to be doing and the overall health of the person.

29. MS 438 Farside family, Brotherton Library, University of Leeds.
30. F.T. Fernie, *Kitchen Physic* (Bristol, 1890), p. 560.
31. Quoted in Audrey Eccles (1982), p. 103.
32. Maria Rundell, *Domestic Cookery* (1851).
33. Ruddock (1926), p. 388.
34. Howard W. Haggard, *Devils Drugs and Doctors* (William Heinemann and Son, 1929), p. 28.
35. Eliza Smith, *The Compleat Housewife or Accomplished Gentlewoman's Companion*, facsimile of the 16th edition of 1758 (Arlon House, King's Langley, 1983), p. 33.
36. Florence White, *Good Things in England* (London: Jonathan Cape, 1932), p. 323.
37. Buchan (1796), p. 16.
38. Cited in Valerie A. Fildes, *Breasts, Bottles and Babies: a history of infant feeding* (Edinburgh: Edinburgh University Press, 1986), p. 288.
39. George Weddel (ed.), *Arcana Fairfaxiana* (Newcastle upon Tyne: Mawson, Swan and Morgan, 1893), p. 51/f. 47.
40. Dr Savory quoted in MS Ripley Castle, 1710.
41. Thomas M. Halsey (ed.), *The Diary of Samuel Sewall* (New York, 1973) vol. I, p. 36, 16 Feb. 1678.
42. William Shakespeare, *A Midsummer Night's Dream*, Act II, scene I, l. 47.
43. Cited in John Brand, *Observations on the Popular Antiquities of Great Britain* (1848, facsimile edition New York: Arms Press, 1970), p. 81.
44. F.R. Raine (ed.), *The Diary of Nicholas Assheton of Downham* (Manchester: Chetham Society, 1848), vol. xiv.
45. John Harland (ed.), *The House and Farm Accounts of the Shuttleworths of Gawthorpe* (Chetham Society, 1868), vol. XLVI, part I, p. 212, notes.
46. Jean Donnison, *Midwives and Medical Men* (London: Heinemann, 1977), p. 45.
47. F.P. Wilson (ed.), *The Batchelar's Banquet* (Oxford: The Clarendon Press, 1929), p. 21.
48. Raines (1848).
49. *The Diary of Nicholas Asheton* (Chetham Society, 1994), xxxi, p. 21, footnote, 'a quotation from an MS diary of Richard Kaye of Baldingstone'.
50. Musacchio (1999).
51. Raphael Holinshed, *Chronicles of England, Scotlande, and Irelande* (London, 1586–7) vol. 2, pp. 807–8.
52. Holinshed (1586–7), pp. 934–5.
53. John Strype, *Memorials of Matters Worthy Remark Ecclesiastical and Civil in the Reign of King Edward VI* (1822) vol. 2, I, p. 6.
54. Harland (1868) vol. XLVI, part I, pp. 212–213. 'Macoro wines' probably indicated macaroons.
55. Harland (1868), p. 224.
56. Wilson (1929), p. 21.
57. Brand (1849), p. 72.
58. Henri Misson, *Memoirs and Observations of His Travels over England*, trans. J. Ozell (London, 1719), p. 35.
59. William Shakespeare, *Famous History of the Life of King Henry VIII* (1612) Act V, Scene iv. This play is a polemical description of the death of Catherine, the marriage of Henry and Anne Boleyn, and Elizabeth's birth.
60. Cited in Brand (1849), p. 81.
61. White (1932), p. 286.
62. Isabella Beeton, *Beeton's Book of Household Management* (facsimile edition, London: Chancellor Press, 1982), p. 854.

63. Lizzie Heritage, *Cassell's Universal Cookbook* (London: Cassell and Company, 1901), pp. 1015, 1019.
64. Edward Pinto, *Treen and other wooden bygones* (Bell and Hyman, 1969), plates 194L, 195B.
65. Isabella Beeton, *The Book of Household Management*, entirely new edition (London: Ward, Lock and Co, 1901), p. 1114.
66. Laura Mason and Catherine Brown, *Traditional Foods of Britain: an inventory* (Totnes: Prospect Books, 1999), p. 201. Traditionally, when the pig was cut up in the autumn, the chine was reserved for the next family christening. Eric Phipps, the butcher who first described this dish to Laura Mason as a christening speciality, fought against legislation in the 1990s which required all food animals to be split down the backbone and have the spinal cord removed. This, a safety measure against the spread of BSE infection is irrelevant for pigs, as they do not suffer from this disease; it also made it impossible for the people of Lincolnshire to maintain their tradition of stuffed chine.
67. Jane Grigson, *Observer Guide to British Cookery* (London: Michael Joseph, 1984), p. 97.
68. Grigson (1984), p. 50.
69. Joseph Wright (ed.), *The English Dialect Dictionary* (Henry Frowde, 1898) vol. 1.
70. *The Gossips Feast or Morrall Tales*, cited in Cressy (1997), p. 168.
71. Brears (1986), pp. 183–4.
72. J. Woodforde, *The Diary of a Country Parson 1758–1802*, ed. J. Beresford (Oxford: Oxford University Press, 1978), pp. 159; 419.
73. Charles Dickens, *Dombey and Son* (1848), ed. Alan Horsman (Oxford: Clarendon Press, 1974), p. 57.
74. Strype (1822), p. 7.
75. Brand (1849), p. 81.
76. Frank Atkinson, *Life and Tradition in Northumberland and Durham* (J.M. Dent and Sons, 1977), p. 149.
77. Cressy (1997), p. 135.
78. Holinshed (1586–7) vol. II, p. 807.
79. Cited in Brand (1849), p. 81.
80. Brears (1987), p. 183.
81. White (1932), p. 323.
82. Trefor M. Owen, *Welsh Folk Customs* (Cardiff: National Museum of Wales, 1978), p. 146.
83. Woodforde (ed. J. Beresford, 1978), p. 604.
84. Cressy (1997) see pp. 167–9.

CHAPTER FOUR

Arvals, Wakes and Month's Minds: Food for Funerals

Peter Brears

Christenings, comings-of-age and marriages all had their ceremonies and communal meals, but none of these were considered to be quite as important as those provided for a funeral. The quality and quantity of the fare provided before, during, and after the funeral were all carefully observed by everyone in the neighbourhood, for it was on this that the reputation and social standing of the family would be judged, whether they be greatest nobles, or the poorest labourers.

Throughout Britain, each locality had its own particular funeral customs. This chapter will concentrate on those which were to be found in most areas from the seventeenth up to the early twentieth centuries, when many funeral meals began to be either arranged by professional caterers, or were strongly influenced by them. We will start before the funeral, and then progress in sequence through the whole series of food- and drink-related ceremonies which followed. This should not be as macabre as might he imagined for, perhaps by way of providing mutual solace, many of these gatherings became positively jolly. 'How like Epicurists do some persons drink at a funeral, as if they were met there to be merry and make it a matter of reioycing that they have got rid of their friends and relations,' wrote one perceptive observer.[1] Similarly those attending late Georgian funerals in Cumberland found that there, as in many other regions, the concourse of visitors rendered the house like a tavern, their noise and tumult being little restrained, and their employment being:

> the drinking of wine and spirits with the smoking of tobacco. The conversation turned, often upon the character of the deceased ... the ordinary topics of the day were discussed ... and each individual, as inclination prompted him, thus maintaining a pretty rapid succession of arrivals and departures, with the exception of, perhaps, one or two who embraced so favourable an opportunity for economical indulgence. 'Where the carcase is, there will the eagles be gathered together.'[2]

Arvals, Wakes and Month's Minds

Ever since people began to make wills to arrange the disposal of their worldly goods, some have also made preparations for their funerals by including instructions for the entertainment of those attending (examples are given below). Others appear to have made rather less formal arrangements; however, one elderly lady living at East Hendred, Oxfordshire, in 1754, specially ordered cold roast beef with beer, ale, and both red and white wines just before she died.[3] The hospitality of a Bradford lady was similarly appreciated by her mourners, one of whom was heard to comment, 'Nice bit o' cake – t' corpse made it!'

Preparations were also made by the family. This is clearly illustrated by an incident which took place near Kirkby Malzeard in Wensleydale around the middle to late nineteenth century. As an old farmer lay dying, the landlord and his lady walked over the moors to enquire about his health, and possibly to see him. The old housewife, who was notoriously mean and miserly, made them a cup of tea, explaining that she was too poor to provide more than simple bread and butter for their entertainment. Unfortunately, this was overheard by a grandchild, who innocently cried, 'Oh grandmother, there's such a beautiful cake in the cupboard,' only to receive the brusque reply, 'Hod thee noise, doant ye know t'cake's for t'burying!'[4]

Whether preparations had been made or not, once death had occurred, ritual and custom would dictate the actions of the bereaved. One important custom, sometimes known as the *Lyke Wake*, is of very great antiquity. 'Waking', or sitting overnight with the corpse, was observed during the period before burial. As early as the mid-fourteenth century the church was finding it necessary to suppress the jovial habits which were then practised at funeral wakes. A provincial synod held in London complained that the ancient and serviceable usage of people gathering together to offer their prayers for the benefit of the dead was becoming overgrown with superstition and turned into an opportunity for theft and debauchery. Therefore, they decreed, none should be allowed to watch over the corpse in a private house except the nearest relatives and friends.[5] Similarly the Council of York, in 1367, forbade 'Those guilty games and follies and all those perverse customs which transformed a house of tears into a house of laughing and excess.'[6]

Needless to say, no-one took any notice of this decree, and wakes continued to be thoroughly enjoyable occasions. Those who wished to be soberly waked still found it necessary to insert instructions in their wills that, 'Ther shall be no yong folkes at my lyke-waike.'[7] As late as 1686, John Aubrey was able to describe how:

> At the funerals in Yorkshire to this day they continue the custom of watching and sitting up all night till the body is interred. In the interim some kneel down and pray by the corpse, some play at cards, some drink, and take tobacco. They have also mimical plays and sports; for example they chose a simple young fellow to be a judge, then the suppliants, having first blacked their hands by rubbing them under the bottom of the pot, beseech his lordship and smut all his face.
>
> The belief in Yorkshire was, among the vulgar (perhaps is in part still) that after the persons death, the soul went over Whinny-moor, and till about 1616–1624 at the funeral, a woman came, like a praefica [an amulet or charm against magic], and sang the following song.[8]

The song, the *Lyke Wake Dirge*, was in fact sung over a corpse at Kildale, in the North Yorkshire Moors, as late as 1800, while local knowledge of its significance, following the soul's journey through purgatory, was still commonplace a century later.[9] It stressed that the most fearsome obstacle, the Flames of Hell, could only be sustained if the deceased had given both food and drink during its lifetime, thus stressing the importance of those life-supporting elements:[10]

> This yah neet, this yah neet,
> Ivvery neet an' awl,
> Fire an' fleet an' cann'l leet,
> An' Christ tak up thi sowl.
>
> Fra t' Brigg o' Dreead 'at thoo mayst pass,
> Ivvery neet an' awl,
> Ti t' fleeams o' Hell thoo'll cum at last,
> An' Christ tak up thi sowl.
>
> If ivver thee gav' owther bite or sup,
> Ivvery neet an' awl,
> T' fleeams 'll nivver catch tha up,
> An' Christ tak up thi sowl.
>
> Bud if bite or sup thou nivver ga' neean,
> Ivvery neet an' awl,
> T' fleeams 'll bo'n tha sair ti' beean
> An Christ tak up thi sowl.

Arvals, Wakes and Month's Minds

In a county celebrated for the quality of its ale for over four centuries, it is not surprising that this strong and fortifying liquor should have become accepted as a traditional part of the hospitality for a wake. One of the most complete accounts of this practice comes from the North Riding town of Helmsley in the late eighteenth or very early nineteenth century when, on the evening preceding a funeral:

> A large fire was made on a brick groundwork [fire grates in cottages were not then in general use]. Near to the fire stood two large puncheons [earthenware bowls] of ale, which had been scalded, and to which herbs and a quantity of sugar had been added. From 20 to 30 persons were generally invited. The oldest men and the best talkers were honoured with a seat in each corner of the fireplace, the others being seated around. Each man, on entering the house, had been invited to go into the room of death to view the remains of some member of the family. On taking his seat, the man had brought before him two silver tankards (kept by ale sellers for such occasions) one containing hot ale, the other cold. The hot was generally preferred. After a few observations on the merit of the deceased, they began the tales of long ago... The tankards were handed round at intervals, accompanied by cakes seasoned like the ale. Cheese accompanied the cakes. Altogether time passed very comfortably, and the wakers departed during the small hours of the morning, no-one being worse for liquor, which, at meetings was only secondary.[11]

A custom sometimes practised before the dead were buried was sin-eating. The most complete account of this is given by John Aubrey:

> In the County of Hereford was an old Custome at funeralls to have poor people, who take upon them all the sinnes of the party deceased. One of them I remember lived in a cottage on Rosse-high way, he was a long, leane, ugly, lamentable poor raskal. The Manner was that when the Corps was brought out of the house and layed on the Biere; a Loafe of bread was brought out, and delivered to the Sinne eater over the corps, as also a Mazar-bowle of maple (Gossips bowle) full of beer, wch. he was to drinke up, and sixpence in money, in consideration whereof he tooke upon him (ipso facto) all the Sinnes of the Defunct, and freed him (or her) from walking after they were dead. This custome alludes

(methinkes) something to the Scape-goat in ye old Laws, Leviticus, cap. XVI, verse 21, 22 … This Custome, (though rarely used in our dayes) yet by some people was observed even in the strictest time of ye Presbyterian goverment; as at Dynder … the kindred of a woman deceased there had this ceremonie punctually performed according to her Will, and also the like was donne at ye City of Hereford in these times, when a woman kept many yeares before her death a Mazard-bowle for the Sinne-eater; and the like in other places in this Countie.[12]

The same custom was practised in Wales at least as late as 1825, when Professor Evans noted a sin-eater at Llanwenoy, Cardiganshire. He was:

abhored by the superstitious as a thing unclean, [he] cut himself off from all social intercourse with his fellow creatures by reason of the life he had chosen; he lived as a rule in a remote place by himself, and those who chanced to meet him avoided him as they would a leper. This unfortunate was held to be the associate of evil spirits, and given to witchcraft, incantations and unholy practices; only when a death took place did they seek him out, and when his purpose was accomplished, they burned the wooden bowl and platter from which he had eaten the food handed across, or placed on the corpse for his consumption.[13]

A similar custom which perhaps had its roots in sin-eating as a communal activity was recorded by Monsieur Jorevin at Shrewsbury in the early 1660s on the occasion of the funeral of a lord:

The relations and friends being assembled in the house of the defunct, the minister advanced into the middle of the chamber where, before the company, he made a funeral oration. It is to be remarked, that during the oration there stood upon the coffin a large pot of wine, out of which everyone drank the health of the deceased. This being finished, six men took up the corpse and carried it on their shoulders to the church.[14]

This would appear to mark the end of a funeral rite which was probably of some considerable antiquity, but yet quite unable to survive into more recent times.

The 'arval', throughout the northern counties of England, was the term for the feast provided for mourners at the end of a funeral. This word is derived directly from the Old Norse *arfr* (inheritance) *öl* (ale, a banquet) as recorded in the Icelandic sagas. In the early tenth century, for example, we can read:

> Thorstein took Thorolf's body to Sweden, and borrowed the earl's hall to drink the arval. He laid Thorolf in the howe with much money to honour him, and the feast was held three nights, according to custom.[15]

It would appear that this practice was introduced into northern England by the Scandinavian settlers of the ninth century, and it was certainly well established by the time that written records became commonplace, five hundred years later. In 1459, for example, James Alanson left an ox for the entertainment of the mourners at his 'arvell', while the earliest Yorkshire dialect glossary, published in York in 1684-5, clearly defines 'An Arvill' as 'a Funeral', and gives the following example of its use in conversation:

> Come bring my Jerkin, Tibb, I'le to'th Arvil,
> Yon man's dead seay seaun, it maks me marvil,
> I thought he leauk'd weel Yesterday at Neaun,
> I little dream'd he wad be dead seay seaun ...
> Wya fare ye weel than, for I'le away,
> They're boon to 'th Kirke, and seay I mun nut stay.[16]

No wonder that the man was in a hurry to get to the arval, for the quality of the entertainment provided for the mourners was always the most lavish that the hosts could possibly afford.

Throughout the medieval period it was customary for a funeral in any great household to be concluded by the provision of a suitably lavish feast. Its purpose was presumably to provide hospitality for those who had travelled some distance to attend the ceremony, as well as to show honour to the dead. Sir Brian de Stapilton of Wighill, who died in 1394, specifically stated in his will that he wished 'the lords, my companions, allies and neighbours, who choose to come and pray for me, and do honour to my poor body, to be made well at ease, and to have enough to drink.'[17] Judging by contemporary household accounts, those attending a medieval funeral feast could be assured of the very best quality, quantity and range of food that was available, as may be seen in the following examples:

Funeral Feast, 1309.[18]

1½ butts of cider	1½ gallons of oysters
5 pigs	2 hogs
1 hare	9 capons
5 sheep	1½ carcases of beef
13 hens	4 bacons
19 geese	

also wine, ale, eggs and bread given to the poor and to friends.

Food eaten at the funeral feast of Lady Katherine Howard, Framlingham Castle, 1465.[19]

2 great boars	48 partridges
12 great oxen	14 pheasants
40 sheep	7 peacocks
12 hogs	36 mallards
70 pigs	36 plovers
12 swans	800 eggs
80 geese	30 gallons of milk
200 conyes	3 gallons of honey
24 capons	32 barrels of beer
140 chickens	3 pipes of wine
30 ducks	

It is clear from these lists that the medieval funeral feast was virtually identical in content to all the other feasts of the period, being founded on a wide variety of cooked meats accompanied by egg-based dishes, all washed down with copious supplies of beer and wine.

In the households of the nobility and wealthier gentry, similar meals continued to be provided up to comparatively recent times. Rather than give a wide selection of menus, however, it might be best to consider one well-documented example in some detail.[20] In June, 1697, Mr. Henry Currer of Kildwick Hall, a splendid stone-built, seventeenth-century mansion overlooking the Aire valley near Skipton in Yorkshire, had to arrange the funeral of his wife Elizabeth. Since he was unsure how to proceed, he immediately took:

> advice with Sister Fothergill abt. Hanging a Room with Mourning, and if soe, what Scutcheons, the Room is 7 Yards Square & whether it be

proper Master & Children should goe to the Church with Corps or not & whether to Cary the Corps in the Coach Carriage like a Herse, or on Four Mens Shoulders under the Paull. Ask if it proper the Mourners goe on foot if the Corps be caryd like on a Hearse. buy Love Ribin to tye the Scarfs.

A Note of things to be bought at York 24 June 97 [mourning costume, gilt clasps for coffin etc].

18 dozen of Naples Rouls of what Largness you think fitt to give. [O]ne a piece[.] Go for large ones
Pickles
    1 Quart of Girkins
    2 Quart of Luke Olives
    1 Quart of Samphire
    1 Quart of pickled Oysters
    3 pound of Anchovies
    2 or 3 pints of other Pickles at G. Folks
2 dozen of Lemons
2 doz. of Oranges
1 large Salmon
6 Lobsters large bought Quick
3 Crabs

Having made this preliminary list, he had to work extremely hard to make all the necessary arrangements for only three days remained before the actual day of the funeral. A further list was next prepared, noting who was to be invited. This was a much more difficult task than might at first be imagined, for everyone had to be placed in a strict social classification which determined what mourning clothing they were to be given, which room they were to occupy, and what quality of entertainment they were to receive. From his detailed lists, we find, in order of precedence: in the Mourning Chamber, were her sisters Ferrand, Endwistle, Fothergill and Pickerin, with black silk mourning; in the Best Chamber, were fifty-seven gentlewomen, leading members of local families, cousins and cousins wives etc. (all of whom had kid gloves) together with nineteen other ladies; in the Purple Chamber, were twenty-one ladies, mainly cousins, cousins' wives etc; downstairs, in the 'Seller Parler', were twenty-nine of the leading gentlemen, including brothers and uncles of the deceased, who all had kid gloves; in the Hall, were thirty-nine gentlemen, a third of them being cousins; in the 'Kitching', were fifty-eight men and women. In addition, there were 22 menservants accompanying the guests, and fourteen more guests still to be invited, making a grand total of 263 guests, all of whom were sent the following invitation:

Sr.
You are desired by Mr. Currer of Kildwick to accompany the Corps of his deceased Wife from his house to the Church upon Tusday the 29 June 97 by eleaven of the Clock in the forenoon.

The food for the funeral feast was now being gathered together, most of the plainer ingredients being obtained from local suppliers, as may be seen in the following accounts:

From Mrs Elinor Jackman at her house in Skipton in Craven in Yorkshire. Bought for Mr. Currer June the 27th, 1697

	s.	d.
40 pounds of Butter at 3½d the pound	11	8
[?] Chickings	1	6¾
5 Chickings	1	3
1 Calfe head	0	6
Calfe feet	0	2
to a Woman per Carying	0	3
	15	4

Mrs Jackman Bill per 15s 4d pd 10 July 1697
Mr Curer acountes for met

	£	s.	d.
for a leg of moton	00	1	2
for [10?] quarter of lam	00	15	00
for 8 quarters of mton	1	14	00
for 2 quarters of vel	00	5	6
for 3 quarters of lam	00	3	9
	2	19	5

5 July 1697 recd…contents of the Bill by me Henery Botomely

	s.	d.
2 Quarters of Mutton	6	0
2 Piggs	6	0
a Turkey	2	0
in all	14	0

Ann Ramsbotham Bill 14s pd. the 3rd of July 97

A p.ticuler of the Charges of Mrs Currer funeral June 29th 1697

	£	s.	d.
To William Lambert per Ale	1	6	0
To Edward Chipindale per Coffin		16	0
To Henry Watson for Wine & Carryage…	8	13	7

Meanwhile, a man on horseback had gone over the moors to Otley, and then on to York, the north of England's main source of gastronomic supplies, this round trip of some 90 miles being necessary to obtain the delicacies required for service to the chief guests in the best rooms:

	£	sh.	d.
June 25th pd. at Yorke per 2 duz. of Lemons	0	6	6
per 2 duz. of Oranges	0	6	0
per a Salmon	0	5	0
per 3 Crabbs	0	2	0
per 8 duz. of Silk Buttons	0	3	0
Per 2 duz. of large Cloth Buttons	0	0	10
pd. per Horse, Oates & Grass	0	2	0
Myself Ordinaries & Extraord.	0	3	3
spent & pd. per Horse at Otley	0	0	9
	1	8	4
July 10 to Andrew B…per gloves	0	10	10
	1	19	2

Bot. of Geo Fothergill 24th June 1697

	£	s.	d.
Imp. na[ples] Bisketts 30lb at 14d and box & cord	1	17	6
per Girkins 1 qt & pott	0	4	2
per Olives 1 qt & pott	0	3	2
per pick. oyster 1 qt & pott	0	3	2
per Anchovies 3½lb & pott at l6d	0	4	2
per Cockles 1 qt & pott	0	2	8
per 2 mangoes & pott	0	3	2
per box & Cord	0	1	6
	2	19	4

noe Rocksamper in Joune
returne 2 Boxes 4s.
Mr Fothergill Bill per Biskett & Pickles, 2 Boxes, 2l. 19s. 4. paid 28 July 97.

Henry Currer Esquire Accounts since June 23d 97.

	£	sh.	d.
Imp. 24lb fine powder sugar at 9d	00	18	00
the 26th per 3lb Curants	00	01	09
the 28th per 1 [?] Sinymon	00	00	10
the 29th per 2 doz glased pipes at	00	00	06

5th July 97 received for the contents of this bill by me James Hargreaves.

Given this detail, it is relatively easy to build up a picture of the catering provided for the mourners at Kildwick on that July morning in 1697. On arriving at the front door of the Hall around 10 a.m., they would have been served with either some of the large Naples biscuits with wine from the cellars below, or with spiced cakes and ale, and then ushered into their respective rooms. Then, at 11 o'clock, they would have walked down the steep hill with the coffin, to attend the service in the long, low church of St Andrew. After the interment they would then make their way slowly back to the Hall, where, ushered once more into their rooms, the servants would proceed to serve the feast.

As in earlier times, its foundation was cooked meat, the beef presumably coming from the Currers' own herd, and the mutton bought in. For those in the best rooms, there would be the turkey and chickens, the pigs and lamb, the salmon, lobsters, crabs, oysters and cockles, all garnished with the expensive pickles from York. The calves' feet would have been boiled and clarified to provide the gelatine base for delicate orange and lemon flavoured jellies; cream and eggs from the Currers' dairy would have provided the ingredients for richly flavoured creams and possets, while the butter, sugar, currants and cinnamon, mixed with the Currers' own flour, would have been baked into spiced cakes for the funeral. As for the veal, it was probably used to make pies, for in the North these were considered to be particularly appropriate for these occasions. At Bowes, for example, it was remembered:

> where ye Arvel Dinner still prevails, the chief and chosen dish at the well-spread board is a rich veal pie, well stored with currants and raisins, and sweet spices. The funeral pie was ate at an early period and is described as being made of 'shrid meates'.[21]

At Bowes, however, the dinners were set out in the middle of the chancel of the church directly after the interment, a great contrast to the crowded and lavish hospitality provided by the Currers of Kildwick.

There is plenty of evidence to suggest that the traditional form of funeral feast continued through to the first quarter of the twentieth century, the following accounts being typical:

Funeral of Benjamin Browne of Troutbeck, 1748.[22]
258 mourners –

	£	sh.	d.
4 dozen Wiggs } 16 dozen of bread	00	04	00
Cakes, 6 dozen at 2d	00	12	00
Beef, a Quart.r.	00	15	06
Veal, a side	00	04	06
Two sheep ... at 6s apiece	00	12	00
Malt, a load [for brewing]	00	07	00
Wine, white & red, 2 gallon	00	17	06
	[3	02	06]

Arvals, Wakes and Month's Minds

Farmer Keld of Whitby's Funeral c. 1760 [23]

9 large hams	15 stone of Cheshire cheese
8 legs of veal	110 dozen penny loaves
20 stone of beef	30 ankers of ale
16 stone of mutton	

John Allin Lister's Funeral Expenses, March, 1822 [24]

	£	sh.	d.
Mr. Hutton's bill, shuggar, currants, lemons etc	1	5	5
Bread 19 doz 19s; beef 6s; expenses 1/2	1	6	2
Paid Mr. Gray for 3½ ankers of ale at 14s per anker	2	9	0
Paid Wm. Thompson for 4½lb of butter, 1/4 per lb.		6	0
Paid Jno. Sumerson for 5st 10¼ lb of chees at 6/5 stone	1	10	4
18lb of gingerbread at 4½d per lb.		6	9
Nutmegs 1/1d; 2lb of butter 1/6 to Robt. Brown		4	1
March 14th: Served 93 poor people with bread and cheese and ale and 47 of them in our own parish receaved 3d each		11	9
	[7	19	6]

Dorothy Agar Rhea's Funeral Expenses, October, 1884 [25]

Ham	20lb	lump shugar	4lb
Pound of beef	24lb	black tea	1lb
Spice bread	24lb	green tea	½lb
chees	10lb	peas	½lb
white bread	12 loaves	tobacco	¼lb
Gingerbread	6lb	100 cards	

In many households the funeral feast was the most expensive meal ever prepared, its scale and richness being quite out of character with the usual round of economical, everyday dinners served to family and friends. In the homes of the poor, too, it was regarded as a point of honour that the mourners should be fed as well as possible, even if it meant going into debt for a considerable time afterwards. On some occasions, the deceased saved up money especially for this purpose, one laundress of 1631:

> [having] reserved out of her labours of life [so much] as will buy some small portion of diet-bread, comfits and burnt claret, to welcome in her neighbours now at her departing, of whose cost they never so freely tasted while she was living.[26]

On others, where the family openly admitted its financial burden, there might be a 'pay berring'. In most parts of Yorkshire these were arranged by having a relative seated by the open coffin to receive a donation from each visitor who came to take a last look at the body before it was committed to the grave. Everyone was expected to give according to their personal circumstances. In other households a collecting basin was placed in a conspicuous position on a table inside the house, wary mourners hovering outside the door to whisper, 'Are the' tackin?' before venturing indoors. The Sheffield custom of being buried 'Hallam fashion' involved every mourner bringing their own bread and cheese and so forth, thus saving the family from considerable expense.[27]

Having considered the funeral feast in general terms, we can now study its individual elements in greater detail, beginning with wine and biscuits. During the Commonwealth, the Common Council of the City of York decided:

> being called to advise touching the great expence of wyne, cakes and banquettinge at funerals in these times of scarcyty…thought fitt and ordered…that no such banquett or expences at all in wine or cakes shall be used hereafter.[28]

As with all such ordinances, it was of course quite ineffectual, and wine appears to have been served at the funerals of the wealthier sections of society from at least the fourteenth century up to the present day. Many of the earlier records refer simply to 'wine', but by the seventeenth century it is being clearly identified as sack, claret, or canary.[29] By the early eighteenth century it was being served hot, Henri Misson noting how:

> Before they set out, and after they return, it is usual to present the guests with something to drink, either red or white wine, boil'd with sugar and Cinnamon, or some such Liquor.[30]

Similarly, W. King's *Art of Cookery in imitation of Horace's Art of Poetry* (1709) records:

> In Northern customs duty was exprest
> To friends departed by their fun'ral feast,
> Tho' I've consulted Hollingshead and Stow,
> I find it very difficult to know
> Who, to refresh th' attendants to the grave
> Burnt claret first, or Naples-bisket gave.

This custom survived in Yorkshire up to the opening of the nineteenth century, after which cold wines, especially port and sherry, became more popular.[31]

In other areas, such as Norfolk, red and white wine, together with chocolate, were served at funerals, as recorded in the diaries of the Reverend James Woodforde. For instance, on 12 February 1782, before the funeral of Mrs Howe at Hockering:

> Before we went to Church there was Chocolate and Toast and Cake with red Wine and white. At half past 11 o'clock we went to Church with the Corpse. ... After our return from Church we had Cake and Wine and Chocolate and dried Toast carried round.[32]

Again, on 25 June 1796, for Mr Bodham's funeral at Mattishall, there were:

> Chocolate, cold Ham, Veal &c. at the side Tables in the Room we were in, the best Parlour.

As for biscuits, they formed an essential part of the funeral entertainment from the early seventeenth century. Samuel Pepys records how, at the funeral of his brother on 18 March 1664, the guests:

> though invited as the custom is about 1 or 2 a-clock, they came not till 4 or 5. But at last, one after another they came – many more than I bid; and by my reconing that I bid 120, but I believe there was nearer 150. Their service was six biscuits apiece, and what they pleased of burnt claret – My Cosen Joyce Norton kept the wine and cakes above – and did give them out to them that served, who had white gloves on.[33]

Biscuits served at funerals came in a variety of shapes, sizes and textures, the most fashionable being the Naples or Savoy variety, made from recipes

Figure 12. A stone mould for funeral biscuits, once in the possession of Thomas Beckwith of York. (Drawing by Peter Brears.)

Figure 13. A sycamore mould for funeral biscuits, once belonging to Mrs Nelson of Burton-in-Lonsdale, now in York Castle Museum. It measures approximately 10 cm (4 inches) across. (Drawing by Peter Brears.)

such as that recorded by Rebecca Price in 1681 as: 'Naple Bisquets; given me at Schoole.'[34] They were made of sugar, almonds, cream, sugar and flour, beaten up, perfumed with rose-water, ambergris and musk and baked in rectangular paper 'coffens' (see recipes, p. 152). These small loaves of biscuit-bread were then sliced into rectangular fingers to form individual funeral biscuits. By the early nineteenth century, the recipe had become greatly simplified, as may be seen in the version published in S.W. Staveley's *New Whole Art of Confectionary* published in Chesterfield in 1816:

FUNERAL BISCUITS
Take twenty-four eggs, three pounds of flour, and three pounds of lump sugar grated, which will make forty eight finger biscuits for a funeral.[35]

By the late nineteenth century they had adopted the form of the crisp sponge-finger biscuits which are still available from confectioners and supermarkets today.

The second quality of funeral biscuit was made from a mixture similar to that of a Scottish shortbread. A stone mould for producing these, once in the possession of Thomas Beckwith of York, illustrated opposite, has a circular recess eleven and a half inches (29 cm) in diameter by a quarter of an inch (0.7 cm) in depth, its face being carved with a heart, a typical local symbol for the soul, the date 1666, and the inscription: 'DIES MORTIS ÆTERNE VITÆ NTALIS EST' (The day of death is the birth of eternal life).[36]

Similar biscuits are recorded throughout the North Riding. In Whitby they are described as a 'round, flat, rather sweet sort of cake biscuit ... lightly sprinkled with sugar, and of a fine even texture within,' while in Upper Wensleydale they were 'round, five to seven inches in diameter and three quarters of an inch thick (price 4d, 6d or 8d) divided into two halves laid together and sealed in a sheet of white paper.'[37] In the Dales they were stamped with a wooden mould such as that illustrated opposite, having a central heart design surrounded by plain circular bands and a zig-zag border; one example used by Mrs Nelson of Longber Farm, Burton-in-Lonsdale, now being in the York Castle Museum, while another from Mrs W.H. Hutchinson of Arkengarthdale is in the Upper Dales Folk Museum at Hawes.[38] Her recipe was a shortbread type, of flour, butter and sugar, with caraway seeds.[39]

The usage of funeral biscuits varied from one area to another. In Whitby in 1817, for example:

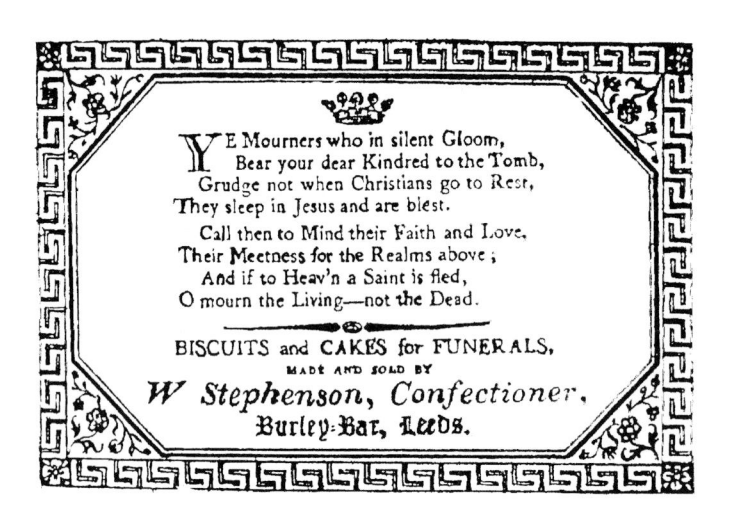

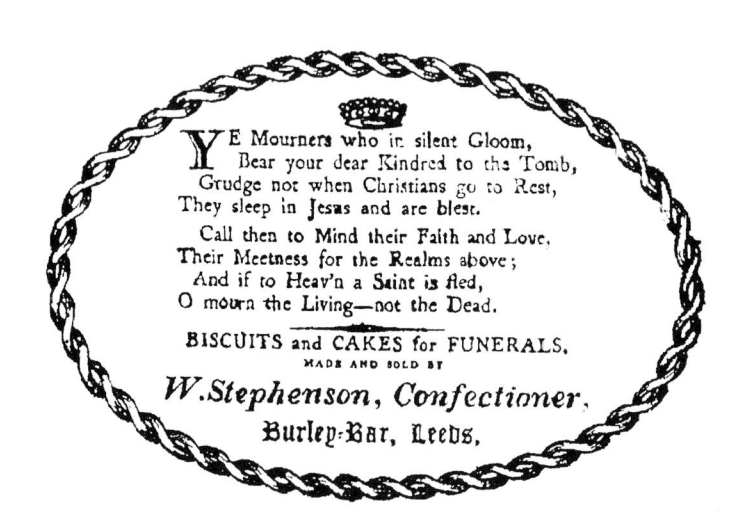

Figure 14. Printed paper wrappers for finger-shaped funeral biscuits. They would have been sealed with black sealing-wax. These were both produced in Leeds around the years 1816–1825.

> Two, three or four females, called servers, distributed wine and sugar-biscuits before the procession moved, and walked before it to the grave, dressed in white, with knots of white ribbons on their left breasts.

In Slaithwaite in the 1860s, 'the invited mourners were met at the door by a person holding a tray containing wine and biscuits, of which they partook before taking their last look at the departed.'[40] In South and West Yorkshire, the biscuits were distributed after the funeral:

> small white paper parcels tied with ribbon, containing two biscuits each, were placed in a basket lined with a white cloth, and a man...went to the house of the friends of the deceased and left one of his little parcels.[41]

At Morpeth in Northumberland they were wrapped in paper and left on a table, so that every person could take a piece with them to the church; while in Lincolnshire the narrow oblong biscuits were served with sherry or port, before the cortege departed.[42] In other parts of the North:

> At the funeral of the richer sort...they had burnt wine and Savoy biscuits, and a paper with two Naples biscuits sealed up to carry home to their families. The paper in which these biscuits were sealed [always with black wax] was printed on one side with a coffin, cross-bone, skulls, hacks, spades, hour-glass etc during the eighteenth century.[43]

Fortunately, a number of wrappers for these biscuits have survived in museums and libraries, perhaps being kept as mementoes of funerals significant to their original collectors. Most date from the early nineteenth century, and provide a graphically lugubrious reminder of this period of high mortality. Usually they bear a printed panel, measuring some 4–5 inches in length by 3–5 inches in width, which was designed to appear nearly on top of the package once the wrappers had been folded and sealed around a pair of biscuits. In the Leeds area the following lines might be printed clockwise around the four sides of the panel:[44]

> I am the Ressurection and the Life,
> He that believeth in me
> Though he were dead, yet shall he live;
> And whosoever liveth, and believeth in me,
> Shall never die. Believest thou this?
> O Death, where is thy Sting?

ARVALS, WAKES AND MONTH'S MINDS

> I am the Resurrection and the Life. He that believeth in me,
>
> O Death where is thy Sting?
>
> WHY should we mourn departing friends
> Or shake when death alarms,
> 'Tis but the voice that Jesus sends,
> To call them to his arms.
>
> The graves of all his saints are blest,
> He soften'd every bed;
> Where should the dying members rest,
> But with their dying head.
>
> BISCUITS AND CAKES FOR FUNERALS,
> MADE AND SOLD BY
> H. Spencer, Confectioner,
> No. 108. *Bottom of Kirkgate*,
> LEEDS.

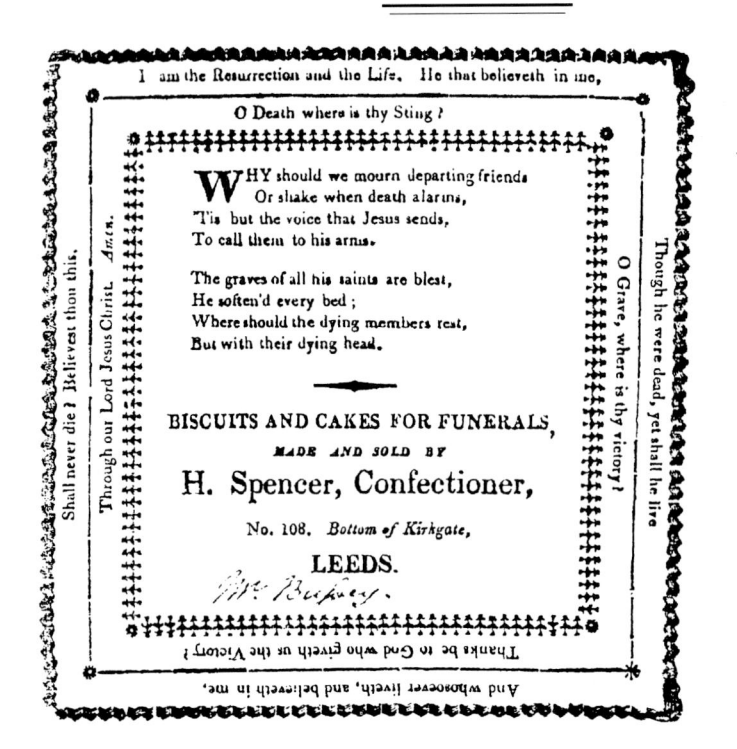

Figure 15. This wrapper for funeral biscuits also dates from approximately 1816–1825.

> I am the Resurrection and the Life. He that believeth in me,
>
> O Grave! Where is thy victory?
>
> "Blessed are the dead who die in the Lord."
>
> DEATH is a friend to all the saints,
>   It calls them to their rest;
> Removes their sorrows and complaints,
>   And ranks them with the blest.
> This awful messenger is come,
>   Commissioned from on high;
> To call me to my native home,
>   That world of perfect joy.
> Farewell, my weeping friends, farewell,
>   My dearest friends, adieu;
> I hope ere long in heaven to dwell,
>   And then I'll welcome you.
> Farewell, my friends, a long farewell,
>   For we shall meet no more;
> Till we are raised with Christ to dwell,
>   On Canaan's happy shore.
>
> E. HUDSON & SON,
> HIGH STREET, GREAT HORTON,
> FUNERALS PROMPTLY ATTENDED TO.

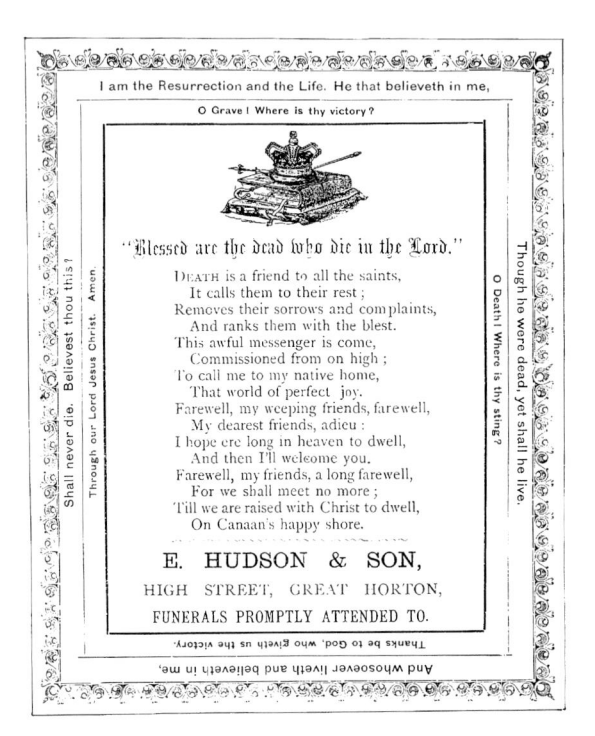

Figure 16. This wrapper for funeral biscuits dates from the late nineteenth century. It comes from Bradford, West Yorkshire and was produced by the undertaker rather than the baker or confectioner.

106

Arvals, Wakes and Month's Minds

> O Grave, where is thy Victory?
> Thanks be to God which giveth us the Victory,
> Through our Lord Jesus Christ.

while in York:[45]

> This trust how certain, when this life is o'er,
> Man dies to live, and lives to die no more.

The central area is reserved for a verse or verses which might celebrate the deceased's joyous reception by his maker, as in M. Wilson's Leeds wrapper:[46]

> Come to Judgement
> Happy soul thy days are ended.
> All thy mourning days below.
> Go, by angel guards attended
> To the sight of Jesus go,
>
> Waiting to receive thy spirit,
> Lo, the Saviour stands above,
> Shews the purchase of his merit
> Reaches out the crown of love,
>
> For the joy he sets before thee
> Bear a momentary pain,
> Die to live a life of glory,
> Suffer with thy Lord to reign.

Hughes and Maudsley preferred to dwell on the resurrection:[47]

> My flesh shall slumber in the ground;
> Till the last trumpet's joyfull sound,
> Then burst the chains with sweet surprise,
> And in my Saviour's image rise.

Most usual of all, however, were stern verses warning the living of their final end, as in the following from Bramley of Halifax (*c.*1790):[48]

> When ghastly Death, with unrelenting hand,
> Cuts down a father! brother! or a friend!
> The still small voice should make you understand,
> How frail you are – how near your final end.

That from A. & M. Heaps of Leeds, which has a particularly unpleasant twist in its tail:[49]

PREPARE TO DIE
Death is a friend to all the Saints,
It calls them to their rest.
Removes their sorrows and complaints
And ranks them with the blest.

This awful messenger is come,
Commissioned from on high
To call me to my native home
That world of perfect joy.

Farewell my weeping friends, farewell,
My dearest friends adieu!
I hope ere long in heaven to dwell
And then I'll welcome you.

Finally, the wrappers bear the name and address of their makers, a convenient form of advertising, together with: 'Biscuits and cakes for funerals', 'made on the shortest notice', or simply the title 'confectioner'. Sometimes other services were offered by the supplier, such as the provision of funeral wines. One of the most unusual suppliers, however, was 'T. Robinson, Surgeon, Settle', who clearly had an eye for business, profitably selling funeral biscuits to the families of those he failed to cure.[50] Elderly informants alive today can still remember the use of funeral biscuits up to the years around the Second World War, but from that time they passed completely out of use, and so are no longer made either in the home or in commercial bakeries.

Cakes of various types, and ale, have played a part in funerals as well as other rites of passage. Ale has probably been the most common drink at funerals in England for over a millennium, although it was relegated to second place in terms of prestige once wine became available. As late as the 1890s Dr Bishop was able to note that 'the quality' had good old port and sponge cake at Wensleydale funerals, while 'the many' had mulled ale and parkin.[51] The consumption of hot or cold ale at wakes has already been described, but it also formed part of the traditional entertainment at the funeral feast, when it usually accompanied spiced buns or cakes.[52]

Arvals, Wakes and Month's Minds

At Dalton-in-Furness in Lancashire (across the sands):

A full meal of bread and cheese and ale was provided at the funeral house, and after the corpse was interred the parish clerk proclaimed at the graveside that the company must repair to some public house. Arrived there, they sat down by fours together, each four being served with two quarts of ale. One half of this was paid for by the conductor of the funeral, and the other half by the company. While they were drinking the ale, a waiter went round with cakes, serving one out to each guest, which he was expected to carry home.

Similarly, in Westmorland, a large table was set out, spread with cheese, wheat-bread and oat-cakes; the ale, either cold or warm according to the season of the year, then being served.[53] In other areas, such as Amersden in Oxfordshire, the ale appears to have fulfilled a rather more ceremonial role, for here, immediately after the burial of every corpse, it was customary to present the minister with a flagon of ale and a cake.[54] Meanwhile, at funeral feasts at Macclesfield in Cheshire, 'funeral cups' (something like coffee cups, but larger) were used for drinking warm beer at funerals.[55]

In Yorkshire, it was customary for a woman serving the ale to wear a clean white linen napkin over her left arm, while the handle of the tankard borne in her right hand was decorated with a piece of lemon peel.[56] In poorer areas, where no silver tankards were available, the large earthenware jugs which took their place for serving the 'berryin' brew' had their rims similarly embellished with lemon peel.[57] Along with many other old-established practices the service of ale in tankards at funerals fell into disuse around the second quarter of the nineteenth century. In the West Yorkshire parish of Mirfield, for example, it had been customary, up to this time, for the long napkins used for carrying the coffin, together with two silver cups (one of them a quart tankard), to be kept at the Hall for the use of the local community. The last time they were lent out, the mistress of the Hall discovered a child dragging one across the fold-yard full of pebbles, upon which, she decided, it was time to stop lending.[58]

Cakes were certainly being eaten at funerals during the sixteenth century, when they were described as 'speysse-bred'.[59] Later accounts give further details of their size and form, those from Kirkby Stephen in Westmorland being made of flour, fruit and spice, and too large to go into a pocket, probably being sufficient for a tea-party for two or three ladies.[60] At

Troutbeck, in the same county, they were 'little buns given to each guest in the open air', the last being distributed here at the funeral of Elizabeth Longmire in 1834.[61] In Yorkshire, this 'arval bread' was made in loaves, spiced with cinnamon, nutmeg, sugar and raisins.[62]

At Eyam in Derbyshire it was the custom to pass around a wicker basket of triangular, spiced, currant cakes to each of the mourners, together with a large tankard of spiced ale, just before the funeral procession set off to the church.[63] Perhaps their recipe was similar to that published by S.W. Staveley in Chesterfield in 1816:[64] a little butter and sugar rubbed into two stones of flour, plus currants, ginger, caraway seeds, cinnamon and rose-water. They were leavened with barm and made 'round at three-pence each', before baking (see recipes, p. 153). A small rectangular loaf made for the funeral of John Alcock, who was buried at Elvaston near Derby on 2 September 1821, was preserved in the Derby museum until quite recently.

An important charitable aspect of funerals was the dole. From the medieval period through to the mid-nineteenth century it was customary, for those who could afford it, to leave money for the distribution of loaves of bread to the poor. Sometimes this took the form of a gift of land with which trustees could raise the necessary resources. The most famous example of this practice comes from the Tichborne family of Hampshire where centuries ago the Lady Mabella, on her death-bed, gained her lord's consent that all the land she could crawl round while carrying a burning billet would be used for this purpose.[65] In the event, she managed to crawl around 23 acres, which are still known as 'The Crawls' to this day. By the eighteenth century it had become customary to bake 1,400 loaves for the dole, each weighing 26 oz., and to give twopence to each additional applicant, after all the loaves were distributed each January, on the Feast of the Annunciation of the Blessed Virgin. It was eventually discontinued in 1796, following complaints from the magistrates and gentry that all the vagabonds, gypsies and idlers of every description who gathered there to collect the dole were pilfering and causing other disturbances throughout the neighbourhood.

Evidence of this practice continuing into relatively modern times, albeit on a more restricted basis, is provided by numerous accounts and descriptions, such as in February 1754, when the Reverend George Woodward of East Hendred, Oxfordshire, notes that, 'the Sunday after [an elderly lady died] a sermon was preached for her, and sixty four people had each of them a twelvepenny loaf.'[66]

Arvals, Wakes and Month's Minds

At Gainsborough in Lincolnshire it was customary to distribute penny loaves on the occasion of a funeral to whosoever demanded them, while at Godeby in Leicestershire the local baker distributed a penny loaf for each member of each household when one of the local community died.[67]

Sometimes these loaves were kept as mementoes of the deceased; Mrs Soar of Elvaston loaning a 400-year-old loaf, reputedly given to her ancestors on the death of one of the Harrington family, to an exhibition held at Kegworth in 1868.[68]

The major funeral feats took place, as already described, on the actual day of the funeral, but on some occasions they might be postponed for a short period, perhaps to enable more people to attend. An illustration of this practice is given in the will of Margaret Atkinson of London, dated 18 October 1544, in which she ordered that on the Sunday after her burial:

> there be provided two dozen of bread, a kilderkin (128 pints) of ale, two gammons of bacon, three shoulders of mutton, and two couple of rabbits, desiring all the parish, as well rich as poor, to take part thereof, and a table to be set in the midst of the church, with everything necessary thereto.[69]

What a splendid gift to her parish! It is very easy to imagine the warm pleasure with which her friends and relations would lay the table in the aisle, complete with its bread, cooked meats and barrel of ale, ready for a communal parish feast to her memory at the end of the divine service.

In England before the Reformation it was also customary to commemorate the deceased by holding a mass on the Menning Day, or Month's Mind, one month after the day of their death; this service was followed by an appropriate feast. Fabyan's *Newe Cronycles*, for example, records that on the death of Sir Robert Chichely, grocer and twice mayor of London, in 1439, he directed in his will:

> upon his Mynde Day a good and competent dyner should be ordeyned unto 24 pore men, and that of housholders of the citee, yf they myght be founde.[70]

Further details of these dinners are given in Fabyan's own will, made 1511. Having instructed his executors to provide sufficient bread, cheese and ale for all those who attended his funeral at the parish church, he further commanded:

Arvals, Wakes and Month's Minds

Ayenst my moneths mynde I will be ordeyned, at the said churche, competent brede, ale, pieces of beffe and moton, and rost rybbys of beefe, and shalbe thought nedeful by the discretion of myn executrice, for all comers to the said obsequy, over and above brede, ale, chese, for the comers unto the dirige over night, And furthermore I will that my said executrice doo purvey ayenst the said moneths mynde 24 peces of beffe and moton, and 24 treen platers, and 24 treen sponyg, which peces of fleshe with the said platers and spoonys, with 24d of silver, I will be yeven unto 24 poore persones of the said parish of Theydon Garnon.[71]

The present of a piece of beef or mutton, a wooden plate and a wooden spoon, together with a whole silver penny, would be greatly appreciated by every one of the poor recipients, and made a suitably charitable end to the donor's funeral rites. During the sixteenth century this final funeral feast appears to have largely fallen out of use, although in rural England the practice of village mourners going dutifully to the parish church for the month's end service still continued into the 1890s.[72]

Arvals, Wakes and Month's Minds

Notes

1. John Brand, *Observations on the Popular Antiquities of Great Britain* (1849), p. 244.
2. William Hone, *The Everyday Book* (1826), I, p. 1077.
3. D. Gibson, (ed.), *A Parson in the Vale of the White Horse* (Gloucester: 1982), p. 54.
4. R.W.S. Bishop, *My Moorland Patients* (1926), p. 159.
5. J. Collier, *Ecclesiastical History* (1840), I, p. 546.
6. B. Puckle, *Funeral Customs* (1926), p. 63.
7. J. Raine, *Wills and Inventories of the Archdeaconry of Richmond* (Surtees Society, 1853), p. 127.
8. John Aubrey, *Remaines of Gentilisme and Judaisme* (1687), reprinted J. Britten (ed.), in *The Publications of the Folk-Lore Society* (1881), IV.
9. W.J Halliday and A.S. Umpleby, *A White Rose Garland* (1949), pp. 185–7.
10. R. Blakeborough, *Yorkshire Wit, Character, Folklore and Custom* (1898), p. 123.
11. I. Cooper, *Helmsley, or Remiscences of 100 Years Ago* (York, c. 1887), p. 37.
12. Aubrey (1687) and *The Gentleman's Magazine* (1822), I, pp. 220–223.
13. Puckle (1926), p. 69.
14. Brand (1849), p. 243.
15. L.W. Faraday, 'Custom and Belief in the Icelandic Sagas', in *Folklore* (1906), LVIII, p. 401.
16. See O.E.D., Ms. Reg. Test. Ebor IV 249b; and G. Meriton, *In Praise of Yorkshire Ale* (1685), 58, 80.
17. H.E. Chetwynd-Stapylton, *The Stapletons of Yorkshire* (1897), p. 132.
18. Puckle (1926), p. 106.
19. The Paston Letters, quoted in M. Girouard, *A Country House Companion* (1987).
20. West Yorkshire Archive Service, Bradford. Currer of Kildwick and Wilson of Eshton MS 68D/82/7/d/37 and 68d/82/26/7; see also P. Brears, *The Compleat Housekeeper: a household in Queen Anne Times* (Wakefield: Wakefield Historical Publications, 2000).
21. J. Hardy, *Denham Tracts* (1631), II, p. 40; and Anon., *Whimsies, or a new cast of characters* (1631), p. 89.
22. W. Rollinson, *Life and Tradition in the Lake District* (1974), p. 53.
23. *Annual Register* (1760).
24. J. Fairfax-Blakeborough, *Yorkshire Days and Yorkshire Ways* (1935), p. 175.
25. Fairfax-Blakeborough (1935), p. 176.
26. Anon., *Whimsies, or a New Cast of Characters* (1631), p. 89.
27. P. Brears, *Traditional Food in Yorkshire* (Edinburgh: John Donald, 1987), p. 189. S.O. Addy, *Glossary of Words Used in the Neighbourhood of Sheffield* (English Dialect Society 'Bidding Funeral', 1886).
28. A. Raine, *Proceedings of the Commonwealth Committee for York and the Ainsty* (Yorkshire Record Series Misc., 1953), IV, CXVIII, p. 27.
29. G.S. Thompson, *Life in a Noble Household 1641–1700* (1937), p. 327.
30. H. Misson, *Memoirs and Observations of His Travels over England*, trans. J. Ozell (London, 1719), p. 88.
31. *The Gentleman's Magazine* (1802), I, p. 105.
32. J. Woodforde, *The Diary of a Country Parson 1758–1802*, ed. J. Beresford (Oxford: Oxford University Press, 1978), 12 Feb 1782 and 25th June 1796; see also 22 May 1771.
33. S. Pepys, *Diary* (18 March 1664).
34. R. Price, *The Compleat Cook* (1681), ed. M. Masson (1974), p. 277.
35. S.W. Staveley, *The New Whole Art of Confectionary* (Chesterfield, 1816), p. 20.
36. *The Gentleman's Magazine* (1802), I, p. 105.
37. Mrs Gutch, *County Folk Lore II; North Riding of Yorkshire & York & the Ainsty* (1889), p. 305.
38. P. Brears, *The Kitchen Catalogue* (York: Castle Museum, 1979), Item 627.

39. M. Hartley, and J. Ingilby, *The Yorkshire Dales* (1963), p. 311.
40. G. Young, *The History of Whitby* (1817), p. 884; J.C. Atkinson, *Slawit in the 'Sixties* (Huddersfield, 1926); and *The Sunday Times* (4 December 1955).
41. C.V. Collier, 'Funeral Biscuits' in *Transactions of the Hunter Archeological Society* (Sheffield, 1929) III.
42. M.C. Balfour, *County Folk Lore IV Northumberland*, ed. N.W. Thomas (1903), p. 100; and E. Gutch, and M.C. Peacock, *County Folk Lore V Lincolnshire* (1908), p. 236.
43. *The Gentleman's Magazine* (1802), I, p. 105.
44. Reprinted in Brears (1987), p. 195.
45. Wrapper of J. Hick, 47 Coney Street, York.
46. Wrapper of M. Wilson, 20 Commercial Street, Leeds, in Leeds City Museums.
47. Wrapper of M. Heaps, 60 Woodhouse Lane, Leeds.
48. Wrapper of Bramley, Confectioner, Tea-Dealer & Milliner, Halifax, c. 1790. Shibden Hall Museum, Halifax.
49. Wrapper of M. Heaps, 60 Woodhouse Lane, Leeds.
50. Wrapper from the funeral of Mrs Oliver, died 7 November 1828, aged 52. Pitt-Rivers Museum, Oxford. Presented by T.G. Burnett, 1919.
51. Bishop (1926).
52. J.H. Nolan (ed.), *Manchester City News* (1880), City Notes and Queries III, p. 232.
53. S.H. Scott, *A Westmoreland Village* (1904), pp. 133–7.
54. W. Andrews (ed.), *Curious Church Customs and Cognate Subjects* (1898), 2nd edition, p. 136.
55. J. Wright, *The English Dialect Dictionary* (1923), 'Funeral'.
56. *The Gentleman's Magazine* (1798), LXVIII, p. 573.
57. A. Wrigley, *Saddleworth Superstitions and Folk Customs* (Oldham, 1904).
58. J.E. Vaux, *Church Folk Lore* (1902), p. 165.
59. J.G. Nichols (ed.), *The Diary of Henry Machin 1550–1563* (Camden Society, 1848), vol. xlii, p. 91.
60. Hardy (1631), p. 54.
61. Scott (1904), p. 137.
62. Wright (1923), 'Arval'.
63. S.O. Addy, *Traditional Tales and Household Remains* (1895), p. 124.
64. Staveley (1816), p. 15.
65. R. Chambers, *The Book of Days* (1866), I, p. 167.
66. Gibson (1982), p. 54.
67. Andrews (1898), p. 135 and The Folk Lore Society, *County Folk Lore* (1895), I, p. 106.
68. *Transactions of the Leicestershire Architectural and Archeological Society* (Leicester, 1868), p. 106.
69. J. Strype (ed.), *Stow's Survey of London* (1791), I, p. 259.
70. Fabyan, *The Newe Cronycles of Englande and of Fraunce* (1513), in Brand (1849), p. 317.
71. Brand (1849), p. 315.
72. *Longman's Magazine* (April 1898), p. 546.

CHAPTER FIVE

FOOD AND DRINK AT IRISH WEDDINGS AND WAKES

Regina Sexton

This paper sets out to examine the nature, role and function of food and drink at Irish weddings and wakes. The focus is limited to those of poor to moderate means in rural Ireland of the nineteenth century and the first half of the twentieth century.[1] This was a particularly formative period in terms of the evolution and diversification of the Irish diet, and the manifestation of these developments on rural food patterns is particularly relevant.

By the second half of the nineteenth century, industrial developments and production improvements, together with a revolution in land and sea transport, brought an array of mass-produced foods to the market. These developments saw an upsurge of commercial activity in small Irish villages and towns and introduced new food choices to those who were hitherto limited to home-produced goods. The prestige and novel status of these goods made them the choice for festive celebrations and special family occasions. As stand-alone items, these goods were of obvious value, but shop-bought ingredients were also increasingly incorporated into home-made foods on special occasions, thus elevating and augmenting their existing status. In particular, the type of baked goods, either acquired or home-produced for weddings and wakes, was directly affected by these developments.

In this respect, the ways in which the shop-bought were assimilated into the running of a self-sufficient, domestic economy are of particular note. Shop-bought goods that demanded little additional preparation, for instance, dominated the wake. On the other hand, wedding fare represents an amalgamation of the acquired with the home-produced. Indeed, in contrast to wake fare, the wedding was largely confined to home-produced ingredients. However, while wedding and wake fare differed in terms of how they were produced, they were both simply prepared and plainly presented.

Furthermore, the fundamental nature of wedding and wake fare was simply an extension of a fundamental attitude to food and cooking in general.

Until well into the twentieth century, economic constraints forced many to continue cooking over the open fire, using a prescribed range of utensils, thereby encouraging a continuation of traditional simple cooking methods using both familiar and novel ingredients. Both are also unified by the fact that they were subservient, in value and importance, to alcoholic beverage, and no wedding or wake was deemed proper without noteworthy quantities of whiskey and porter.

Apart from exploring the nature of Irish wedding and wake fare, this paper will also place both in a wider social context, with additional attention to the well-defined rituals and symbolism that such food and drink evoked.

Marriage: the location of the wedding feast

The location of the wedding feast and, indeed, the organization and unfolding of the entire wedding day were governed by various factors, but until well into the twentieth century they were routinely set in a domestic context. In the earlier parts of the nineteenth century, this was encouraged by the fact that, in many cases, the wedding party did not travel to church at all and instead, 'the priest would have come to the house and performed the ceremony there'.[2] Occasionally, the nuptial vows were exchanged in the house in which the couple would live, which was most commonly the groom's, or his parent's house. However, Mr and Mrs Hall, in describing the nature of the Irish wedding in the early nineteenth century, seem to suggest that locating the feast in the bride's house was conditional on the economic comfort of her immediate male relatives. They note:

> If the bride's father or brother be a 'strong' farmer, who can afford to furnish a good dinner, the marriage takes place at the bride's house, the bridegroom bringing with him as many of his friends as he choose to accompany him.[3]

In addition, what is interesting to note is that often the period of celebration was not delayed until the formalities of the religious ceremony were complete, but rather they began in the bride's house on the wedding morning. Even when church ceremonies became more commonplace, the wedding day continued to be marked by two very defined periods of celebration, in which food and drink were extended to family and the wider community. In outlining the marriage customs in Kilgarvin in County Kerry one informant states:

> Up to about the end of the first quarter of the present century the wedding party used to begin at the bride's home early in the morning. All the guests used to arrive in side-cars, common carts and saddle horses. They feasted until it was time for the young couple to go to the chapel. The young man would, of course, be present at the bride's house, but both he and the bride would travel in separate vehicles until they were married, when they would go from the chapel to the young man's home in the same conveyance.[4]

Another informant from County Galway recalls similar practice:

> There would be another party after the wedding at the groom's house besides the one before the wedding at the bride's house.[5]

That the morning celebrations were clearly fixed within the bride's domain is supported by the nineteenth-century Irish writer William Carleton. In his highly stylised account of a typical nineteenth-century rural wedding, *Shane Fadh's Wedding*, he offers the following footnote:

> The morning, or the early part of the day, on which the Irish couple are married, up until noon, is called the bride's part, which, if the fortunes of the pair are to be happy, is expected to be fair – rain or storm being considered indicative of future calamity.[6]

In the body of the story itself, the morning festivities centre around the 'bride's breakfast', which was lavishly supplied with boiled and roasted meats and poteen, and was hugely attended by both the bride's and groom's party before they departed for church:

> here we all sat down; myself and my next relations in the bride's house, and the others in the barn and garden; for one house wouldn't hold the half of us.[7]

The tone of the story does little to disguise the fact that the church ceremony was merely a temporary, though necessary, diversion in a well-planned day of merriment. And, while this sentiment may have been deliberately worked by Carleton to augment his quaint, if not comic, style, it does nonetheless highlight the reality that the religious ceremony was not the most important part of the day, but simply the focal point that divided it into two clear periods of celebration. In addition, the often colourful procession to church was the impetus for the movement of the celebrations from the bride's house to that of the groom.

Indeed, the movement of guests and feasting from the bride's to the groom's house celebrated not only the enjoining of the young couple, but it also dramatised the conventions that attended many weddings in rural Ireland of the late nineteenth and early twentieth centuries. Such conventions, based on an arranged or match-made union, demanded that the bride – along with her negotiated dowry in the form of land, money or other property – should take up residence with the groom and his family. On a more personal level, the journey represented the changing fortunes of the bride, her advance to adult status and her elevation to the main woman of the house in her groom's holding.

The movement of festivities from one house to another therefore celebrated the cementing of new social and economic alliances, the preservation and augmentation of land holdings and the future extension and continuation of the family unit that was sure to follow, by the careful selection of a young, fertile bride. It also established a new pecking order in the running of the domestic economy.

If, on the other hand, the married couple were of more mature years, or if the groom were forced to delay marriage, as was increasingly the pattern in post-famine rural Ireland,[8] then the couple might opt to celebrate the union with a small, intimate, family gathering in one of the many unsophisticated restaurants, or 'eatin' houses', that flourished in the cities or small rural towns. Martin Morrissey, in describing life in west County Galway in the 1940s, recalls the marriage day of a local farmer in his fifties:

> It was a quiet wedding and after the ceremony the small group had a meal in a restaurant, better known as an 'eating house'. That was the grand total of their honeymoon.[9]

Here the fare was plain and simple, but wholesome and substantial and similar to that provided at home, with fried and boiled meats dominating the menu.[10] These small-scale celebrations were designed to minimize the social scrutiny that invariably attended the marriage of a mature couple or the marriage of a couple where the groom was greatly separated in years from his young bride. The latter were often the object of mockery and derision within small rural communities and the desire to celebrate their union at a distance from their home base went some way towards preserving their dignity. But, however effective in protecting the couple, the tenor of the celebrations was at variance from routine practice, in that it discouraged large-scale community participation in the event.

Generally speaking, Irish weddings were diligently attended as a matter of course and social duty. The occasion of a marriage and the ensuing celebrations were greatly anticipated and served to satisfy the entertainment needs of not only the family members and friends, but also of the entire community. Robbing the neighbours of their day out was therefore viewed as an exercise in social exclusion, albeit by the few against the majority, which compounded and justified popular preoccupation with the more unusual wedding.

ACCOMMODATING AND PROVISIONING THE WEDDING

For those who went the conventional route, the large wedding celebration brought its own package of problems. In particular, accommodating and provisioning the sheer volume of guests, from a practical and economical perspective, were important concerns. To accommodate the numbers, the house, together with appropriate farmyard buildings and the garden, if the weather was clement, were organized for the wedding feast. 'Often,' says Danaher, 'there was not room in the house for the throng, and tables were laid in the barn, or even in the farmyard.'[11] Within these designate areas, guests were carefully grouped and seated in accordance with their social status. The antiquarian Thomas Crofton Croker, writing in the early nineteenth century, explains:

> A house with three contiguous apartments is selected for a wedding; the reason of this is to preserve a distinction between the classes of company expected. The best apartment is reserved for the bride and the bridegroom, the priest, the piper, and the most opulent and respectable guests, as the landlord, his family and neighbouring gentry, who are always invited and usually attend on such occasions. The second apartment is appropriated for the neighbours in general; and the third, or an out-house, is devoted to the reception of buckaughs, shulers, and other beggars.[12]

Croker's observations identify the piper and the priest as the most important guests outside family members and this reflects a value system that placed the merits of the religious and the musician on an equal footing; the former sanctified the day but the latter ensured its lively continuation from early morning until the following day. Furthermore, Croker's additional statement that, 'When the marriage is celebrated two collections are raised amongst the guests, the first for the priest, the other for the piper,'[13] indicates that their contributions were considered indispensable to the proper functioning of the wedding day and, accordingly, their special status imbued with certain dining privileges.

The special treatment of select guests was also detectable in respect of table dressing, distribution of food and access to cutlery. Robert Bell, an Englishman who travelled through Ireland at the beginning of the nineteenth century, and stands as one of the more balanced social commentators, observed:

> The chief personage at this entertainment was the parish Priest, or his deputy. The next in pre-eminence was the Squire: but it was not every country gentlemen who could attain the honour of being present...at a wedding feast: if he had not resided long in the neighbourhood; if he had not by a gentle and familiar deportment, but above all, by conversing with the peasants in the Irish language, commanded their esteem, and conciliated their affections, he would not have been invited. The Squire, however, could have been easily dispensed with: but, next to the Priest, the Musician was the most necessary person to render the entertainment complete. He was generally a performer on the bagpipes; and the host was often obliged to send for one to the distance of near 20 or 30 miles. Doors taken off the hinges and laid on benches, constituted a dinner table, of which no part was covered with a cloth expect the head: here the Priest sat as president or lord over all the guests, and had the most delicate of the viands placed before him. The others sat in order according to their rank; which was estimated by the consideration of their property, their age, and their reputation. The meat was usually cut into pieces about the size of brickbats, and placed along the table in large wooden platters, out of which the guests helped themselves often without the aid of knives or forks: for the few instruments of this kind which could be procured, were appropriated to the service of the Priest and the select party whom he chose to honour with his conversation.[14]

Food and Drink at Irish Weddings and Wakes

What is important to note from Bell's description is that this is a broad stroke of rural pre-famine Ireland where adverse poverty levels made fundamental household items – cutlery, table linen and even the kitchen table – unaffordable and unattainable luxuries for a sizeable proportion of the population. Indeed, these may also be viewed as unnecessary luxuries, since the potato- and buttermilk-dominated diet of the small farmer and landless labourer was easily prepared and consumed with the most fundamental of equipment. The potatoes were simply boiled in an open pot, and strained in a wicker basket. After straining, the potatoes were routinely left in the basket which, in the absence of a table, was placed on the floor, sometimes on top of the butter churn, from which potatoes were selected and eaten by the family and guests, with bare hands. Hence the wedding feast outlined by Bell and the generosity of the host and hostess, of whom he says, 'instead of sitting down to dinner, waited upon the … company and pressed … them to eat with an earnestness and familiarity that would have been highly disgusting to persons of more refined manners,'[15] should, in the context of its time, be taken as a gesture of extravagance.

Wedding fare

The overt simplicity evident in Bell's description of the wedding feast above also extends to Irish wedding fare in general, where an abundance of boiled meats and a profusion of potatoes with garden vegetables was the order of the day. Again Bell supplies the detail:

> The dinner, which was the only meal on this occasion, generally consisted of mutton, salt pork, bacon and poultry; with an abundance of potatoes and common garden vegetables.[16]

While Carleton's description of an Irish rural wedding feast seems to confirm Bell's observations:

> Such lashins of corned beef, and rounds of beef, and legs of mutton, and bacon – turkeys and geese, and barn-door fowls, young and fat. They may talk as they will, but commend me to a piece of good ould bacon, ate with crock butther, and phaties, and cabbage. Sure enough, they leathered away at everything, but this and the pudding were the favourites. … There was half-a-dozen gorsoons [young boys] carrying about the beer in cans, with froth upon it like barm – but that was beer in airnest.[17]

But while Irish wedding fare was plain, simply prepared and home-produced – Bell makes the point that, 'no part of the fare was purchased by money except the whiskey or beer'[18] – the abundance of the table and the generosity of the host offset the banality of the event. Exaggerated hospitality was expected on such occasions and if not forthcoming the reputation of the host was damaged in the wider community. In order to protect the standing of the economically pressed, close neighbours discreetly contributed gifts of food. Danaher explains:

> if it was known that a very large crowd would gather, tactful neighbours had helped things on with presents of fowl, bacon, bread, cakes, and beverages, for any appearance of shortage or niggardliness at a wedding was a source of shame for all concerned, and might be 'thrown up against them' by some ill-intentioned person at a fair or a market years afterwards.[19]

In addition, these food offerings came with the understanding that if the gift-givers were similarly strained at some point in the future, they could call or rely upon the reciprocation of help.

Any retrospective judgement about the simple and plain nature of wedding fare must be tempered with consideration of the everyday diet. Sir John Carr, a Devonshire gentleman writing of Ireland in the early nineteenth century, reminds us that in the climate of a potato-dominated diet, a piece of meat with vegetables was a relished treat saved for Sundays and special celebratory occasions:

> the family live upon potatoes and butter-milk six days in the week, and instead of 'an added pudding', the Sabbath is generally celebrated by bacon and greens.[20]

Nor was a heavy potato diet exclusively associated with the pre-famine period. Granted, in post-famine Ireland, the potato failed to regain its former status: improved living standards gave many the opportunity of diversifying their diet, and meat and fat intake rose accordingly. However, in some quarters potatoes and milk continued as meal stalwarts, as revealed in a survey conducted by schoolgirls in 1976 in County Mayo. The girls interviewed elderly people around the Ballina area of County Mayo about past food habits. Here the informants, mostly housewives, farmers and fishermen, offered information they had heard from their own parents and neighbours in the community. In summary, they concluded:

> In this area potatoes were almost their only food. Bread, meat, and tea were treats reserved for the great feasts of Christmas and Easter. Breakfast [was] potatoes and milk unless he had a chance to buy a hundred of meal, then they had stirabout when the potatoes got bad. For dinner and sometimes supper they might have fish. Milk was not always available.[21]

And while the food was plain and devoid of elaborately prepared dishes and, indeed, very often limited to a single dish, the aspiration to set it apart for the special occasion was expressed in other ways. The diverse choice of fresh meat and fowl that was offered on such occasions must be considered as indulgent. Fresh meat was a luxury reserved for festive occasions and it came as a welcome change from the more commonly consumed, salted varieties, most notably salted beef and pork.

Until well into the twentieth century such fare characterized the Irish rural wedding banquet. And while guests recognized the simplicity of the fare they were also apt to acknowledge that it was highly valued and appreciated, as one County Waterford informant indicates:

> and as to the food, nobody worried about huge wedding-cakes or elaborate dishes. A couple of barm-bracks or currant cakes or a sweet loaf, and plenty of boiled bacon or mutton and fowl, which everybody with a little bit of a farm could produce, were then the order of the day; and because these things were only to be had in 'plentiness' or rare occasions people enjoyed them all the more, and seldom found fault if there was nothing better.[22]

The wedding-cake

If Irish rural wedding fare was plain and simple and largely home-produced, then it is reasonable to expect that the choice and type of wedding-cake should be bound by similar constraints. Many of the sources for the period list oatcakes,[23] currant cakes,[24] treacle cakes,[25] sweet bread,[26] raisin loaves,[27] boxty bread,[28] porter cakes[29] and barm bracks[30] as the most popular choices. What is immediately striking about this array is that few can be technically classified as cakes; rather, most are enriched breads, representing a variation and improvement on the bread of everyday use. A number, notably oatcakes and boxty bread, are also the products of self-sufficient domestic economy.

Both are also clearly associated with specific regions: oatcakes, for example, although widespread before the introduction of the potato, lingered as an important part of the diet in northern and north-western counties; while boxty bread was largely, though not exclusively, confined to the north-midland and north-west-midland counties. The nature of the rural Irish wedding-cake/bread was, therefore, no different from wedding fare in general; it was plain, easily and quickly prepared in a domestic context, sometimes regionally variable and often dependent on the available home-produced ingredients to hand.

But, however unsophisticated, the wedding 'cake' did evolve and undergo improvement throughout the nineteenth century, due in part to the introduction of sodium bicarbonate and potassium bitartrate[31] in the first half of that century.

When combined with buttermilk or sour milk, sodium bicarbonate (and often a combination of bread soda and cream of tartar) worked as an effective and reliable leaven, even in the presence of home-grown wheat which, owing to the country's damp climate, was notoriously unpredictable in bread-making. Until the introduction of this new leavening agent, rural Ireland did not have a very pronounced domestic tradition in producing yeast-leavened wheaten loaves. Indeed, the fact that an enclosed, built-up wall oven was not a standard feature in all households, together with the variable quality of Irish wheat, militated against the emergence of that tradition. Even with limited baking utensils and working with an open fire, the arrival of sodium bicarbonate and its union with buttermilk made the production of successful soda bread a reality for those who had the requisite ingredients and equipment.

As the nineteenth century progressed, wheaten soda became the standard daily bread. And, as this bread stales quickly, a tradition was soon established which saw the woman of the house preparing a fresh soda each day. In fact, offering up anything but bread of the same day's baking was considered an insult and a sure sign of careless hospitality and poor housekeeping.

For festive occasions, both religious and secular, and for occasions of family celebration, this bread was called into service, though its status was elevated for special times by the inclusion of luxury, shop-bought ingredients – sugar, dried fruit, treacle and, occasionally, caraway seeds. Therefore, references to sweet cake, raisin bread, currant cake and treacle cake must be interpreted as fancy versions of the basic soda cake. To expect anything different, however, would not be reasonable, given the nature of inherited baking skills and the capabilities of the rural kitchen. Neither extended to the production of tiered and iced wedding-cakes; a reality that is expressed in sentiments like, 'As for a wedding-cake, there might have been a big treacle cake instead of the fancy iced cake of today.'[32]

And while rudimentary in nature, these were a marked improvement on the more traditional bread varieties, in particular, flat cakes of oats and barley that were often abrasive, and palatable only in the presence of copious quantities of butter. Accordingly, in many regions, the growing popularity of soda cakes displaced these older staples and, by extension, threatened their role as the choice baked product for weddings and similarly important occasions. This older reliance on cakes of oats and barley invariably made them the choice for weddings,[33] particularly for those who could not afford the more prestigious wheaten varieties. Indeed, a cake of oats, however ordinary, was selected for the wedding feast at a County Derry ceremony in 1835 and here it was labelled the 'bridecake'.[34]

However, the term 'bridecake' does not simply refer to the special status of the cake baked for the wedding feast, but rather it alluded more specifically to the practice of breaking the cake over the bride's head. In Ireland, this custom was well established in a band of counties running from County Louth on the east coast to County Sligo on the west.[35] It was also widespread in County Galway. It was not, however, unique to Ireland and the practice is well attested in England and Scotland.[36] Many Irish accounts indicate that the cake was broken over the bride as she entered her new home, a point of transition symbolizing her imminent role as the first woman of the house. To emphasis the symbolism of her changing status, her mother-in-law was often seen to hand the fire-tongs or churn-dash. Ó Danachair elaborates:

> In some places the old woman handed her new daughter-in-law the tongs and invited her to adjust the fire on the open hearth. In others the dash-churn, symbol of her control of butter-making, was put in her hand as well as the tongs.[37]

No doubt, the obvious phallic nature of these household items may have indirectly and symbolically suggested the question of fertility. In addition, these ritualistic gestures left little doubt as to her future household activities in dominating the work of the kitchen and also, perhaps, in dominating any other female occupants. One County Cavan informant described the mélange of sentiments that must have occupied the bride's mother-in-law as she welcomed her home for the first time. After the breaking of the cake ceremony:

> The mother-in-law embraced and kissed her, but the old lady viewed her closely for some time – from a distance, of course – and tried to ascertain from her appearance, manner and behaviour what sort of woman her son had 'tied himself to for better or for worse'. The old lady was also thinking of herself – she was anxious to know from the bride's demeanour and her 'manner of speech' the sort of woman that would be on the floor with her for the remainder of her days.[38]

In contrast to these procedures, the cake was often broken after the wedding feast as the bride sat at the table,[39] or stood amongst the gathered assembly.[40] Alternatively, the cake might broken by attendant guests who then threw bits at the bride, a variation that is highly reminiscent of the custom of throwing wheat, rice or confetti, suggesting that the practice may have been bound up with the question of fertility. However, those informants who could remember witnessing or hearing of this ritual understood that it was enacted with the wish that the bride would not want or go hungry.[41]

If the cake was broken over the bride's head, slices or pieces were often distributed amongst the guests;[42] but if the cake were crumbled for throwing, this was not an option. Instead, young, unmarried girls, who subsequently saved them to dream upon, eagerly seized upon the crumbs that fell to the floor. The understanding was that such dreams would reveal the identity of their future husbands.[43] That such totems were popular seems to be suggested by Carleton's rather enigmatic anecdote. He describes how, after the cake was distributed amongst the guests, the friar rolled up his allowance in a piece of paper and proclaimed:

> I'll have good fun...dividing this to-morrow among the *colleens* [young girls] when I'm collecting my oats...but I'll make them give me the worth of it something, if it was only a fat hen or a square of bacon.[44]

A variation of the sale of the wedding-cake, enacted for different results, was seen at the wedding celebrations held in south Armagh at the turn of the twentieth century as, 'the priest arose and went around with the bridecake which he sold in pieces to the men and women present.' In this example, the sale was designed to make up the priest's fee.[45] That such a procedure enjoyed some antiquity is clear from Mr and Mrs Hall's description of a rural Irish wedding in the early nineteenth century:

> the priest marries the young couple, and then the bridecake is brought in and placed before the priest, who, putting on his stole, blesses it, and cuts it into small slices, which are handed round on a large dish among the guests, generally by one of the coadjutors. Each guest takes a slice of cake, and lays down in place of it a donation for the priest, consisting of pounds, crowns, or shillings, according to the ability of the donor.[46]

As noted above, it was customary, particularly amongst the less affluent classes, for guests to contribute gifts of food for the wedding feast; and this contribution was a further gesture of community participation in easing the economic strain of the wedding day.

Drink

It is safe to say, and the evidence supports the observation, that consumption of alcoholic beverage, music and dancing, were the most pronounced features of an Irish wedding and heartily enjoyed, even more so than the wedding banquet. In the earlier period, whiskey and wine were the preserves of the wealthier classes, but by the nineteenth century whiskey, and later still porter, were widely available to all, becoming a routine feature of Irish weddings.

The strong association between drink and weddings – and indeed wakes and christenings – was strengthened from the late eighteenth century, owing to a number of revenue amendments and industrial improvements. The Revenue Act of 1779, for example, banned small stills and imposed a minimum duty on others, thereby forcing small-scale distillation underground. As a result, illicit distillation grew rapidly, providing even the least affluent with an abundance of cheap, illegal liquor or poteen.

Even with the suppression of many illicit stills after the 1860s, owing to better law enforcement, the consolidation of the larger urban distillers and improvements in the quality and taste of their produce satisfied market demands. In addition, excise duty on beer was abolished in 1795, thereby reducing costs; while throughout the nineteenth century the quality of Irish barley, together with improvement in malting and brewing techniques, resulted in a dramatic extension of markets. With the opening of the railways in the post-famine period, these new market changes had their effect upon rural Ireland. Easy access to whiskey, illicit or otherwise, and beer made alcohol a standard part of all festivities. 'There was drinking and feasting,' recalls one County Waterford informant, 'but then unlike the present time drink, and enough of it, "to set the whole houseful singing," could be had for a few shillings'.[47]

Indeed, the fact that drink fuelled singing and dancing and night-long entertainment made it a crucial and inevitable part of any successful gathering. The host was obliged not only to provide ample hospitality as described above, but also to ensure that the guests were sufficiently provided to maximize entertainment and, indeed, to partake in prolonging the festivities well into the night. In this sense, the Irish wedding was designed not only to celebrate a marriage union but also functioned as one of the highlights in the often bereft social calendar of rural communities. The sense of personal enjoyment that weddings brought to individual guests is evident in the following account of wedding festivities in County Cavan:

> A wedding was a big event in the social life of the people of rural Ireland and, to quote an old time song, 'The Night of the Wedding was The night of the Fun'. ... There was no shortage of musicians – there were flute players, fiddlers and melodian or concertina players, and they all 'took their turn' and 'kept the music going'. The dancing was kept with great enthusiasm, and many of the older people 'took a hand at the fun'. ... A half-door was taken off its hinges and placed 'on its flat' in the middle of the floor. This was the usual form of 'dancing-deck' at rural dances and weddings, and was placed there for the step-dancers. ... Old men and women of seventy years and over were often seen to 'take to the boards' with a skill and agility that would do credit to boys and girls in their teens. ... Tea was served a couple of times during the night, while the bottle and glass 'went round' at intervals. In later years there were two or three half barrels of porter. This was filled into a large sized gallon which was carried by one man, while another man served out the porter in mugs. If there was a prolonged interval before the next 'round' some thirsty soul could be heard saying: 'I wonder what is keeping them with the gallon.'[48]

The interdependence between alcohol, enjoyment and entertainment demanded that all beverage be dispensed in an organized, though liberal, fashion and accordingly one man, often a friend of the family, was appointed to see after the affair and distribute the drink as it was needed. He was expected to be familiar with each guest's tastes and in turn press them to drink heartily.[49]

Very often, however, the drinking rituals began before the formal celebrations and the so-called 'race for the bottle' is a defined and widespread feature of the Irish wedding tradition.[50] The following account, recorded in 1941, is typical. Incidentally, it is interesting to speculate that the bride's participation may be related to, or may be a variation of, the custom of breaking the cake over her head, and it may have been an extravagant gesture, signalling that this was her day and one that marked her passage to her new role as wife and housekeeper:

> An event of much importance at weddings in by-gone days was 'The Race for the Bottle'. This was a five-naggin bottle of whiskey or poteen that was kept specially for the purpose in the home of 'the groom'. About a mile or half mile from 'The Wedding House' the party came to a halt. The 'fastest running horses' were unyoked and taken out of their respective vehicles. They were then mounted by their owners, and at a given signal they raced for the 'groom's' house. The first to arrive was the winner of the bottle. He was met outside and handed his trophy. He then turned and raced back in triumph to where the remainder of the party were waiting. Amid ringing cheers, he handed the bottle to the bride who pulled the cork, tasted the contents or pretended to do so, and then gave the bottle to her husband who drank a little of the liquor. It was then passed around till it 'went as far as it could go'. It was next returned to the bride who jumped down off the car and smashed it against a stone on the side of the road. In some cases a number of young men ran on foot for 'the bottle'. This being over, the party continued their journey to the home of the newly married couple.[51]

Drink also served as an attraction which drew outside performers and musicians to the wedding celebrations. Groups of singers and musicians, called 'strawboys', came to the house to offer alternative entertainment and to toast the married couple with whiskey and porter. Outside the northern counties, the custom of 'strawing the wedding' was well attested and has been adequately describe and discussed elsewhere.[52] The following account should suffice in outlining the general picture:

Food and Drink at Irish Weddings and Wakes

One of the events of the night was the arrival of the un-invited guests – the 'straw-men' or 'granues'. Their coming being signalised by the cheers which they gave in the yard or street, and their cries of 'Long live the bride and groom'. They were all disguised. On many occasions they had bundles of straw woven round their bodies and covering their faces, so that they could not be recognised by anyone. In some instances they wore multi-coloured garments, false faces and 'comical shaped' hats. The object of their visit was to get a mug or two of porter or a glass or two of whiskey.[53]

The duration and prolonged nature of the wedding, caused by the fusion of drink and entertainment, are some of its most enduring and characteristic features; and the early nineteenth-century observation by Croker, 'that festivities seldom conclude before day-break the next morning,'[54] also holds true for the contemporary practice.[55]

Wakes

In Ireland, wakes, particularly those of the less affluent, were boisterous social affairs, characterized by an abundance of drink and, to a lesser extent, by food, with merriment and lively entertainment in the form of riotous, but organized and highly stylized, wake-games. Wakes, notes Seán Ó Súilleabháin, 'were far merrier than weddings.'[56] They were intended to give family, neighbours and friends the opportunity to pay last respects and to sympathize with the bereaved. Food and drink fortified those who had travelled long distances and sustained those who waked the corpse throughout the night.

But food did not serve solely as a vehicle for welcoming, entertaining and sustaining the mourners; rather the liberal distribution of such augmented the good reputation of the deceased. However, it is clear that the acquisition of alcoholic beverage, and plenty of it, was the foremost concern. It was offered in stupendous quantities at the wake and often carried to the graveyard, sometimes with unsavoury consequences. Food, on the other hand, was of a limited variety and few funeral specialities existed. It was, like Irish rural wedding fare described above, plain and simple, though they were certain conventions as to the procuring of the funeral provisions and the distribution throughout the night.

Food and Drink at Irish Weddings and Wakes

Providing for the Wake

The fact that wakes were numerously attended, and with great gusto on behalf of the mourners, meant that provisioning the night often severely compromised the economic standing of the bereaved family and, as a result, many could be left near-destitute. One account from the letters of the Blake family of Renvyle House in Connemara, written in the early 1820s, addresses the hardship that ensued:

> These wakes are attended with great, and to the poor, with serious expense, which is another strong objection to the custom. Often do the children of a peasant spend more, on this occasion, in the purchase of tobacco, tea, and whiskey, with all the other requisites of a decent funeral, than is earned by them for many a long month after. It is not an uncommon thing for a fund to be reserved for this purpose by the parent himself: and many is the guinea which, in these times of extreme distress, has been reluctantly produced in aid of a starving family, from the precious hoard.[57]

Popular attendance at wakes was for the obvious reason of sympathizing and paying last respects, but many were also drawn to the social and communal dimensions. Mr and Mrs Hall, writing of their tour of Ireland in the early 1840s, note:

> The funerals are invariably attended by a numerous concourse; some from affection to the deceased; others, as a tribute of respect to a neighbour; and a large proportion, because time is of small value, and a day unemployed is not looked upon in the light of money lost.[58]

In face of such gatherings, it was imperative to maintain the good reputation of the deceased and, as Croker points out, in the early nineteenth century, 'an easy death and a fine funeral,'[59] weighed heavily on the minds of the elderly before death. In life, this morbid concern with 'a fine send off' meant that many denied themselves and their families the necessities of life. For those without the support of family and friends, the fear of a poor and ill-planned funeral was even more pronounced. Again Croker notes:

> When advanced in life, it is usual, particularly with those who are destitute and friendless, to deny themselves the common necessaries of

life and to hoard up every trifle they can collect for the expenses of their wake and funeral.[60]

This longing for a good send off responded to a basic human desire to preserve and boost the deceased's reputation on this final and finite occasion. As in many societies, the lavish distribution of food and drink at the wake was a means of maintaining the dignity of the deceased, while at the same time strengthening the good standing of the deceased's family in the community.

Funeral foods

It could be said that Irish funeral food was overwhelmingly unremarkable. The sources are awash with references to the energy and money spent in acquiring and consuming alcoholic beverage. Food, if mentioned at all, is covered in blanket terms. In this respect, Carleton's observation that, 'The best of aiting and dhrinking that they can afford is provided,'[61] is typical of these scant treatments. However, by the late nineteenth century, a clearer picture begins to emerge: by this time, a standard funeral package of goods was established and demanded that bread, ideally shop-bought,[62] together with butter and jam,[63] and occasionally ham[64] and biscuits,[65] be offered to mourners. Tea[66] and sugar[67] – for making a hot, sweet beverage – were equally standard. Essentially, therefore, mourners were welcomed and their expressions of sympathy acknowledged with a light meal of bread and butter and jam, taken with sweet tea. In more affluent circumstances, a cold meal of ham and loaf bread with butter and jam was offered.

That these items are now household staples should not obscure the fact that in the second half of the nineteenth century these were luxury novel provisions befitting special occasions. To those confined to the taste of home-produced foods, anything shop-bought must have been utterly desirable, if not hugely fashionable. Furthermore, the fact that these goods were acquired with hard-earned cash, or else exchanged at the grocer's for items which demanded the woman of the house employ effort in their production (like eggs or butter), satisfied both the expectations of the mourners and the social duty of the family in providing quality hospitality.

These goods were also the product of a wider set of commercial and infrastructure developments that began to change the nature, and indeed the diet, of rural Ireland from the second half of the nineteenth century onwards. An upsurge in the availability and demand for commercially-produced goods was facilitated by the spread of a new railway network. Consequently, the distribution of groceries throughout rural Ireland increased and grocers' shops mushroomed in small Irish rural villages and towns. In addition, the importation of cheaper, American wheat encouraged the emergence of many new bakeries and brought a flood of white, yeast-leavened bread to the market.

The novelty value attached to shop-bought commercial goods, in particular white, yeast bread, and tea, jam and sugar, established them as desirable items of their time. The repeated late-nineteenth-century references to the purchase of white baker's bread, together with sugar, jam and tea for the wake night might, at first glance, seem blandly insignificant but, in light of the commercial developments described above, it is clear that these were held in great esteem and valued above anything the woman of the house could produce. To offer mourners shop-bought bread in place of everyday, domestically produced breads is significant and is evidence of the aspiration, at least, to acquire a speciality, baked product for the occasion.

But while factory breads were prestige items, they were not exclusively associated with the wake. They were, in fact, present at most festive occasions of importance, or offered to guests of high standing in the community.[68] However, two baked products that are specifically designated 'funeral' foods are funeral buns and funeral biscuits. To date, I have come across just one reference to funeral buns and four to funeral biscuits and I am indebted to Myrtle Allen for sending recipes for both. In communication, she says:

> When I was collecting traditional Irish recipes for the *Irish Farmers' Journal* in the late '60s, I was sent a recipe for funeral buns and funeral biscuits. The buns are more like a bread or a brack, only 1 lb of butter to 2 stone of flour, 1 lb sugar, 3 lbs currants, ginger, seeds, cinnamon to taste and rose water mixed with milk. [The informant, a Mrs Marie Kelly from County Carlow] says that this makes 48 cakes, each weighting a lb before baking, and costing three old pennies. Mrs. Kelly says that about 130 years ago funeral buns were a great favourite and were always given to mourners at wakes and funerals. They were, of course, washed down with lashings of whiskey which was as easily given then as tea is now.
>
> The funeral biscuits have lots of eggs, 2 dozen to 3 lbs of flour, and 3 lbs of lump-sugar grated. The informant says that this recipe dates from 1834 and she adds, serve with a tumbler of whiskey.[69]

Other recipes for funeral biscuits are enlivened with currants and caraway seeds. The use of expensive ingredients – butter, lots of eggs, dried fruit and spices[70] – affirms their special taste and status, while the shape of these funeral goods is also significant. All are hand-size, suitable for easy and comfortable eating, especially if trying to manage a tumbler or mug in the other hand.

Just two additional references to biscuits in a funeral or wake context have come to light, although in both cases they are not specifically termed 'funeral' biscuits. One informant states:

> When the Rosary is said and someone goes to town to order a coffin and get a habit and get the priest to bless it. He also brings Whiskey, Wine, Biscuits, Bread, butter, Jam, Snuff, Plug tobacco, and white clay pipes.[71]

This suggests that biscuits could also be shop-bought, but whether they were of a specific type cannot be ascertained. It may also be suggested that the offering of biscuits, at times, might have been limited to, or more closely associated with, female mourners. Another informant states that after prayers the men repaired to the kitchen for refreshments while, 'the women folk usually remain in the room where the corpse is laid out and refreshments such as wine and biscuits are handed round to them.'[72]

The fact that biscuits were dainty morsels in comparison to bulkier slices of loaf bread may have deemed them more suitable for female consumption. Alternatively, the type of beverage chosen by mourners may also have determined the nature of the accompanying food.

Certain conventions also attended the procuring of the wake goods, which were variously known as 'the funeral goods'[73] or 'the funeral charges'.[74] As soon as death was imminent, 'when the fingers and nose goes cold,'[75] says one informant, a family member, usually male, made the journey to the nearest town to buy the necessities. Often the journey was made in company of a friend or neighbour.[76] Indeed, an air of superstition surrounded this ritual which saw that one person never travelled alone.[77] One County Kerry informant colours the picture:

> My father went to Kilgarvan for the groceries, pipes and tobacco and other 'preparations'. He was accompanied by a neighbour as they say it isn't right for anyone to go alone in the night for preparations for a wake, for a priest for a dying person, or for a midwife in a case of childbirth.[78]

At times, the travelling companion was often a woman of the locality,[79] and it is possible that female participation in this instance was necessary to insure that the bereaved male family member made an informed choice when it came to purchasing the food.

The routine of distributing food at the wake varied, but generally it did not begin until the welcoming gestures of hospitality were complete. Mourners were welcomed with tobacco-filled clay pipes. Drinks, mostly whiskey and porter, and sometimes wine for the women, went around but the variety and volume varied with available economic funds. When these formalities were complete, eating commenced, and as mourners arrived to pay their respects, they were ushered to the table to partake in the fare. And this pattern continued, with round after round of mourners coming to the table, until all the company was satisfied.[80] Tea and bread, with butter and jam, were offered once or twice during the night,[81] or in accordance with the ability of the bereaved, to the mourners who waked the corpse, while at the break of day another meal was offered.[82]

The setting of the funeral fare was also an important concern, as the corpse was often laid out on what, in many cases, was the household's only table. Such circumstances forced an improvised solution, like the one witnessed by the Blasket Island writer, Tomás O'Crohan, at a wake he attended on the mainland:

> four women jumped up and laid down a door lid across two stools, and before long I saw all the crockery in the house put together and arranged on the door. Soon I saw two pots of tea coming to the edge of the ashes, two women carrying one, and one the other. They put tea into them and filled them up with boiling water till the two were full to the brim. The other two women were bringing white bread till the door lid was covered all over.[83]

In less affluent households, mourners, conscious of the economic burdens that wake would impose, abstained from food to ensure that those who had travelled long distances had their fill, and in general mourners who lived in the locality ate lightly, if at all, with the same considerations in mind.[84] When, for example, Tomás O'Crohan attended the above mentioned wake on the mainland in Dunquin, he was already some days away from his island home and weary from attending a pig market in nearby Dingle. With these considerations in mind, the man of the house advised him to take his share of the food saying, 'You're not like the rest. They're beside their own home, but you are some way from yours.'[85]

In some areas material left after the wake, whether, food, drink, tobacco or snuff, was never consumed in the house of the bereaved but instead given to neighbours or the wandering poor.[86] Lady Wilde, writing in the late nineteenth century, states that for some nights after the wake it was also customary to leave food for the departed spirits:

> It is a very general custom during some nights after a death to leave food outside the house – a griddle cake or a dish of potatoes. If it is gone in the morning the spirits must have taken it; for no human being would touch the food left for the dead.[87]

Alcoholic beverages at wakes

For many, however, the food dimension to the wake was merely incidental and the lure of free drink was the main attraction. Again, Tomás O' Crohan highlights this reality in his description of an island:

> Those with a fondness for drink had no interest whatever in the food. Drink, not food, was what suited them, for parching thirst was their trouble, not hunger. Accordingly, they made for the corner where the barrel of porter was set up and turned their backs on the part of the kitchen where the table was laid out. Four pints were poured for every man that round.[88]

Here, there is a tangible sense of disregard for the food, as if partaking in it was a waste of valuable drinking time.

The free availability of drink must also account for the numerous attendants at wakes referred to above, and inevitably led to a stream of mourners whose interest was more in securing beverage than in sympathizing with the bereaved. Carleton draws attention to this tendency towards injurious hospitality in noting that, 'there is generally open house, for it's unknown how people injure themselves by their kindness and waste at christenings, weddings, and wakes.'[89]

The excessive quantity of drink taken at wakes is a feature of note and one that astounded contemporary commentators and visitors to the island. Similar to Carleton's observation, they were struck by the consequences of excessive generosity. Seán Ó Súilleabháin refers to the County Tyrone clergyman, Thomas Campbell, and his 1776 account of wakes in the south of Ireland, noting:

> That the consumption of whiskey was such that Campbell thought, the relatives of the deceased would be impoverished for evermore. He told of a poor woman who had laid by a few guineas to cover her own burial expenses, and who started to beg in order that those few guineas might remain intact to supply the neighbours with plenty of whiskey and tobacco at her wake and funeral.[90]

Similarly William Hamilton Maxwell, writing of his attendance at a wake in the early nineteenth century, observes that 'Whiskey [was present], in quantities passing all understanding.'[91] The generous distribution of drink was fuelled by the low cost of illicit whiskey. Indeed, according to one County Cork informant, wakes and weddings played no small part in sustaining the illicit distillation industry. He makes the case:

> The people in general were in good circumstances about that time and drink was cheap. Also in some districts the potheen maker made 'a haul out of a funeral and wake'.[92]

Apart from serving as an expression of hospitality, alcoholic beverage aided in prolonging the entertainment and in guaranteeing that the wake was the enjoyable social event that mourners had come to expect. It would be incorrect, if not irresponsible, however, to maintain that the sense of fun and frolic that characterized so many rural wakes in former times was a standard feature. Rather, the prevailing atmosphere was dictated by the circumstances of the deceased's departure from life. Tragic occurrences of death — that of a child, a youth cut down in the prime of life or the death of a parent that left needy dependants — were marked with behaviour befitting their solemnity. In these circumstances, the communal partaking in alcoholic beverage was part of the grieving process that anaesthetized pain and served as a temporary release in the initial period of profound anguish.

From a practical perspective, drink was also occasionally distributed in the graveyard as a mark of gratitude to those members of the community who attended the corpse, opened the grave and bore the coffin.[93]

As a little 'dropeen' was always brought to the graveyard for near friends and the grave diggers...[94] A drop of whiskey is given to people who place the dead in the coffin and those engaged at the grave.[95]

For those who chose to enact the practice, these final libations symbolically marked the close of the funeral rites, as one County Cork informant recalls:

it was shared out at the graveyard gate when all was over and both bottle and glass thrown back into the graveyard when finished with. These should on no account be taken home.[96]

As might be expected, such extravagances irked the conservative middle classes and drew repeated criticism from the Catholic clergy and hierarchy, who were repulsed by the often lewd and immoral behaviour that followed these revellers. In the earlier periods, episcopal synods continuously issued directives forbidding the consumption of alcohol at wakes and funerals, in an attempt to curb such abuses; while in the nineteenth and early twentieth centuries individual bishops saw fit to take up the cause.[97] Their persistence did eventually pay off, but nonetheless drink continued to endure as an established part of the Irish wake, but present in more conservative quantities.

Conclusion

At the risk of sounding repetitive, it must be emphasized that wedding and wake fare was plain and simple, and often inferior in status to alcoholic beverage, but this should not obscure the fact that special efforts were employed to set it apart – an abundance of meats at the wedding, for example, or the acquisition of prestige goods for the wake. For both these occasions, choosing specific baked goods was of distinct concern. This is particularly evident in the existence of wake specialities, in the form of wake buns and biscuits.

In all, then, the feast was a well-defined feature of the Irish rural wedding and wake in the nineteenth and early-twentieth centuries, where the food was unpretentious but plentiful and but one facet of a broader pattern of often injuriously generous hospitality. For the less affluent, this tendency towards extravagant expenditure at crucial life junctures was a means of reaffirming their good reputation as generous and upstanding members of the community. The extension of good hospitality in times of grief and celebration can therefore be viewed as a way of renewing their membership, so to speak, of the wider social group. Fulfilling this predetermined social duty was also an investment for future times and imbued them with certain rights. It could justify their calls for help and assistance, be they emotional or practical, laborious or spiritual. If nothing else, their plentiful offerings of food and drink guaranteed that in turn they would be included in similar events.

Both weddings and wakes created the opportunity for the community to operate as a whole, where the partaking in shared food and drink served to preserved social bonds and strengthen the internal workings of a closely knit group.

FOOD AND DRINK AT IRISH WEDDINGS AND WAKES

NOTES

1. A considerable body of material relating to twentieth-century Ireland has been taken from the archives of the Irish Folklore Commission (hereafter I.F.C.). This was a state-funded body established in 1935. Part-time and full-time collectors recorded material on popular custom, tradition and belief. The commission was disbanded in 1971, but its work is carried on by the Department of Irish Folklore at University College, Dublin. Its archives are housed in this department. The material taken from the archive is published here by the kind permission of the Head of the Department of Irish Folklore, University College, Dublin.
2. K. Danaher, *In Ireland Long Ago* (Cork, 1978, first published 1962), p. 154.
3. Mr and Mrs S. C. Hall, *Ireland, Its Scenery and Character* (London, 1842), p. 164.
4. I.F.C. 608: 462.
5. I.F.C. 1839: 195–196.
6. W. Carleton, *Traits and Stories of the Irish Peasantry* (Buckinghamshire, 1990), vol. 1 & 2 (first published in 23 parts, 1842–44), 1, p. 60.
7. Carleton (1990), p. 62.
8. The pattern of delayed or postponed marriage has been comprehensively detailed by C. Curtain, 'Marriage and Family', in *Ireland: A Sociological Profile*, ed. Patrick Clancy, Sheelagh Drudy, Kathleen Lynch and Liam O' Dowd (Dublin, 1986), pp. 155–172.
9. M. Morrissey, *Land of My Cradle Days. Recollections from a Country Childhood* (Dublin, 1991), p. 125.
10. As their no-nonsense name suggests, these 'eating houses' served no-nonsense plain and solid food. They were part of the small-town landscape until well into the twentieth century. They were particularly busy on fair and market days when animal drovers and buyers flocked into towns from surrounding rural areas. Here, hungry men took comfort in hearty and familiar meals. Pers. comm. Meehaul Magner, Mallow, County Cork; see also, for example, O' Donnell, *The Days of the Servant Boy* (Cork, 1997), p. 133.
11. Danaher (1978), p. 154.
12. T.C. Croker, *Researches in the South of Ireland* (London, 1824), p. 235. For the special treatment of select guests see also Hall (1842), p. 165.
13. Croker (1824), p. 235.
14. A. Hadfield and J. McVeogh (eds.), *Strangers to that Land. British Perceptions of Ireland from the Reformation to the Famine* (Buckinghamshire, 1994), p. 211.
15. Hadfield and McVeogh (1994), p. 211.
16. Hadfield and McVeogh (1994), p. 210.
17. Carleton (1990), 1, p. 71.
18. Hadfield and McVeogh (1994), p. 211.
19. Danaher (1978), p. 154.
20. J. Carr *The Stranger in Ireland* (Shannon, 1970, first published London, 1806), p. 152.
21. I.F.C. 1884: 42.
22. I.F.C. 466–467.
23. L.M. Ballard, *Forgetting Frolic. Marriage Traditions in Ireland* (Belfast, 1998), p. 112; C. Ó Danachair, 'Some marriage customs and their regional distribution', in *Béaloideas, iml* (1974–1976), p. 155.
24. I.F.C. 466–467.
25. K. Concannon (ed.), *Inishbofin Through Time and Tide* (Inishbofin, 1993), p. 77.
26. I.F.C. 466–467.
27. I.F.C. 608: 450.
28. I.F.C. 1884: 154. Boxty is a variety of potato bread made variously with grated raw potato, mashed potato, flour and baking soda. After the dough was mixed, using varying

combinations of the listed ingredients, it was baked on the pan or griddle. Boiled boxty or boxty dumplings were also popular. Boxty bread and boxty dumplings were notably associated with the food patterns of the midland counties of Ireland.

29. I.F.C. 1884: 154.
30. I.F.C. 466–467.
31. C. Ó Danachair, 'Bread in Ireland', in *Food in Perspective*. eds. Alexander Fenton and Trefor M. Owen (Edinburgh, 1981), p. 65.
32. K. Concannon (1993), p. 77.
33. Ó Danachair (1974–1976), p. 155.
34. Ballard (1998), p. 112.
35. Ó Danachair (1974–1976), pp. 151–155.
36. I. Opie and M. Tatem (eds.), *A Dictionary of Superstitions* (Oxford, 1992), pp. 435–436.
37. Ó Danachair (1974–76), p. 151.
38. I.F.C. 791: 368.
39. Ballard (1998), p. 112.
40. Carleton (1990), 1, p. 79.
41. A similar ritual was also enacted on New Year's Eve in an attempt to banish hunger from the house for the following year. This tradition of 'beating out the hunger' with the aid or a loaf or a cake of bread was widespread and, while the intent behind the symbolism was the same in all areas, what differed were the details of execution. The following summary of the New Year's Eve custom was recorded in the Barony of Imokilly, in East Cork, in 1937: 'A cake was thrown against the door by the man or woman of the house to keep hunger away from the house during the following year. The person who performed the operation said while doing so: "Buailfimíd an gorta amach [we'll beat out hunger]." Or, crumbs were thrown at the doors and windows "to show that no one was hungry" – this was done by persons who went from house to house of set purpose to do so. The direction of the wind was noticed: an east wind on that night boded ill to Ireland.' Some hit the bread against the front or back door, while others threw the loaf out the door, sometimes to the accompaniment of various chants. See S. Ó Súilleabháin, 'Some folklore traditions of Imokilly', in *Journal of the Cork Historical and Archaeological Society* (1945), part 2, vol. L, No. 172, p. 77.
42. Carleton (1990), 1, p. 79.
43. Ó Danachair (1974–1976), p. 155.
44. Carleton (1990), 1, p. 79.
45. Ballard (1998), p. 113.
46. Hall (1842), p. 165.
47. I.F.C. 466.
48. I.F.C. 791: 369–372.
49. Danaher (1978), p. 156.
50. Ó Danachair (1974–1976), p. 142–148.
51. I.F.C. 791: 365–366.
52. Ó Danachair (1974–1976), p. 156–163.
53. I.F.C. 791: 373.
54. Croker (1824), p. 235.
55. Indeed, I was recently amused to read Darina Allen's tongue-in-cheek appraisal of the differences in duration between English and Irish weddings. She writes: 'English weddings are quite a different sort of occasion to Irish weddings, the posher the wedding the more genteel it tends to be. Lots of sipping champagne in morning suits and then suddenly, it's all over. The sudden end is very baffling for Irish people accustomed to a wedding going on for at least a day and a night.' *The Examiner* (Cork, 27 February 1997).
56. Ó Súilleabháin (1997), p. 26.

57. K. Whelan (ed.), *Letters from the Irish Highlands of Connemara. By the Blake Family of Renvyle House (1823–1824)* (Clifden, 1995), p. 157.
58. Hall (1842), pp. 230–231.
59. Croker (1824), p. 166.
60. Croker (1824), p. 166.
61. Carleton (1990), 1, p. 113.
62. I.F.C. 791: 381; 581: 301; 608: 334; 549: 206, 219, 218; 550: 46. T. O' Crohan, *The Islandman* (Oxford, 1951, first published 1937), p. 213; T. O' Crohan, *Island Cross-Talk. Pages from a Blasket Island Diary* (Oxford, 1986, first published 1928), p. 101.
63. I.F.C. 549: 206, 219, 218. E. Cross, *The Tailor and Ansty* (Cork, 1970), p. 67; O' Crohan (1951), p. 213; O' Crohan (1986), p. 101.
64. I.F.C. 549: 218, 219; D. Allen, *Irish Traditional Cooking* (London, 1995), p. 123.
65. I.F.C. 549: 206, 328.
66. I.F.C. 791: 381; 581: 301; 608: 334; 549: 218, 219; 550: 46; O' Crohan (1951), p. 213; O' Crohan (1986), p. 101.
67. I.F.C. 791: 381; 581: 301; 549: 219; 550: 46.
68. For example, white baker's bread was often referred to as 'priest's bread' because white bread was purchased to mark the occasion of the priest's visit to the house. Similarly, this type of bread was also purchased for the breakfast that proceeded or the meal that followed the Station mass. The Station mass was an annual event amongst rural communities when mass was celebrated in a local house. Parishioners took it in turns to host the mass and they also provided food for the celebratory meal that followed. The priest was the honoured guest on these occasions and great attention was paid to preparing his plate and procuring the best quality ingredients for his meal.
69. M. Allen, personal comment. Also compare the recipe for 'Funeral Buns' (recipes, p. 153), and the biscuits quoted above by Brears, p. 101ff.
70. M. Allen, personal comment.
71. I.F.C. 549: 206.
72. I.F.C. 549: 328.
73. I.F.C. 791: 381.
74. I.F.C. 581: 301.
75. I.F.C. 549: 206.
76. I.F.C. 549: 222; 791: 381; O' Crohan (1951), p. 208.
77. I.F.C. 1839: 133.
78. I.F.C. 608: 333.
79. O' Crohan (1951), p. 206.
80. O' Crohan (1951) and I.F.C. 608: 334.
81. I.F.C. 549: 206.
82. O' Crohan (1951), p. 213.
83. O' Crohan (1951), pp. 209–210.
84. O' Crohan (1951), p. 213 and I.F.C. 1839: 133.
85. O' Crohan (1951), p. 213.
86. Danaher (1978), p. 174.
87. Lady Wilde, *Quaint Irish Customs and Superstitions* (Cork, 1988), pp. 35–36.
88. O' Crohan (1951), p. 101.
89. Carleton (1990), 1, p. 113.
90. Ó Súilleabháin (1997), pp. 17–18.
91. W.H. Maxwell, *Wild Sports of the West of Ireland* (Southampton, 1986, first published 1832), p. 256.
92. I.F.C. 550: 87.
93. I.F.C. 581: 309–310.
94. I.F.C. 550: 69.
95. I.F.C. 550: 88.
96. I.F.C. 550: 69.
97. See, for example, Ó Súilleabháin (1997), 19–23.

CHAPTER SIX

RECIPES

TO MAKE A MARCHPANE
(Sir Hugh Platt, 1609)

Take two pounds of Almonds beeing blaunched and dryed in a sieue ouer the fire, beate them in a stone mortar, and when they be small mix with them two pound of sugar being finely beaten, adding two or three spoonfulls of Rosewater, and that will keep your almonds from oiling: when your paste is beaten fine, driue it thin with a rowling pin, and so lay it on a bottome of wafers, then raise vp a little edge on the side, and so bake it, then yce it with Rosewater and Sugar, then put it in the ouen againe, and when you see your yce is risen vp and drie, then take it out of the Ouen and garnish it with prettie conceipts, as birds & beastes beeing cast out of standing moulds. Sticke long comfits vpright in it, cast bisket and carowaies in it, and so seure it; gild it before your seure it: you may also print off this Marchpane paste in your moulds for banqueting dishes. And of this paste our comfit makers at this day make their letters, knots, Armes, escocheons, beasts, birds and other fancies.[1]

THE COUNTESS OF RUTLANDS RECEIPT FOR MAKING THE RARE BANBURY CAKE, WHICH WAS SO MUCH PRAISED AT HER DAUGHTERS
(THE RIGHT HONOURABLE THE LADY CHAWORTHS) WEDDING
(W.M., 1658)

Take a peck of fine flower, and half an ounce of large Mace, half an ounce of Nutmegs, and half an ounce of Cinnamon, your Cinnamon and Nutmegs must be sifted through a Searce, two pounds of Butter, half a score of Egges, put out four of the whites of them, something above a pint of good Ale-yeast, beate your Eggs very well and straine them with your Yeast, and a little warme water into your flowre, and stirre them together, then put your butter cold in little Lumpes: The water you knead withall must be scalding hot, if you will make it good past, the which having done, lay the paste to rise in a warm Cloth a quarter of an hour, or thereupon; then put in ten pounds of Currans, and a little Muske and Ambergreece dissolved in Rosewater, your Currans must be made very dry, or else they will make your Cake heavy, strew as much Sugar finely beaten amongst the Currans, as you shall think the water hath taken away the sweetnesse from them; break your past into little pieces, into a kimnell or such like thing, and lay a Layer of past broken into little pieces, and a layer of Currans, untill your Currans are all put in, mingle the past and the Currans very well, but take heed of breaking the Currans, you must take out a piece of past after it hath risen in a warme cloth before you put in the Currans to cover the top, and the bottom, you must roule the cover something thin, and the bottom likewise, and wet it with Rosewater, and close them at the bottom of the side, or the middle which you like best, prick the top and the sides with a small long Pin; when your Cake is ready to go into the Oven, cut it in the midst of the side round about with a knife an inch deep, if your Cake be of a peck of Meale, it must stand two hours in the Oven, your Oven must be as hot as for Manchet.[2]

To Make Hypocras
(W.M., 1655)

Take four Gallons of Claret Wine, eight ounces of Cinnamon, three Oranges, of Ginger, Cloves and Nutmegs a small quantity, Sugar six pound, three sprigs of Rosemary, bruise all the spices somewhat small, and so put them into the Wine, and keep them close stopped, and often shaked together a day or two, then let it run through a gelly bag twice or thrice with a quart of new Milk.[3]

To make a Rock in Sweet-Meats
(Hannah Woolley, 1674)

First take a flat broad voiding Basket; then have in readiness a good thick Plum Cake, then cut your Cake fit to the bottom of the Basket, and cut a hole in the middle of it, that the foot of your Glass may go in, which must be a Fountain-Glass, let it be as high a one as you can get; put the foot of it in the hole of the Cake edgling that it may stand the faster, then tie the Cake fast with a Tape to the Basket, first cross one way and then another, then tie the foot of the Glass in that manner too, that it may stand steady, then cut some odd holes in your Cake carelesly, then take some Gum Dragon steeped in Rosewater, and mix it with some fine Sugar, not too thick, and with that you must fasten all your Rock together, in these holes which you cut in your Cake you must fasten some sort of Biskets, as Naples Biskets, and other common Bisket made long, and some ragged, and some coloured, that they may look like great ill-favoured, Stones, and some handsome, some long, some short, some bigger, and some lesser, as you know Nature doth afford, and some of one colour and some of another, let some stand upright and some aslaunt, and some quite along, and fasten them all with your Gum, then put in some better Sweet-meats, as Mackeroons and Marchpanes, carelesly made as to the shape, and not put on the Rock in a set form, also some rough Almond Cakes made with the long slices of Almonds (as I have directed before;) so build it up in this manner, and fasten it with the Gum and Sugar, till it be very high, then in some places you must put whole Quinces Candied, both red and white, whole Orange Pills and Limon Pills Candied; dried Apricocks, Pears and Pippins Candied, whole Peaches Candied, then set up here and there great lumps of brown and white Sugar-candy upon the stick, which much resembles some clusters of fine Stones growing on a Rock; for Sand which lies sometimes among the little Stones, strew some brown Sugar; for Moss, take herbs of a Rock Candy; then you must make the likeness of Snakes and Snails and Worms, and of any venomous Creature you can think of; make them in Sugar Plate and colour them to their likeness, and put them in the holes that they may seem to lurk, and some Snails creeping one way and some other; then take all manner of Comfits, both rough and smooth, both great and small, and colour many of them, some of one colour and some of another, let some be white and some speckled, then when you have coloured them, and that they are dry, mix them together and throw them into the Crests, but not too many in one place, for that will hide the shape of your work, then throw in some Chips of all sorts of Fruit Candied, as Orange, Limon, Citron, Quince, Pear, and Apples, for of all these you may make Chips; then all manner of dryed Plumbs, and Cherries, Cornelions dryed, Rasps and Currans; and in some places throw a few Prunelles, Pistachio Nuts, blanched Almonds, Pine Kernels, or any such like, and a pound of the great round perfumed Comfits; then take the lid off the top of the Glass and fill it with preserved Grapes, and fill another with some Harts-horn Jelly, place these two far from one another, and if you let some kind of Fowl, made in Marchpanes, as a Peacock, or such like, and some right Feathers gummed on with Gum Arabick; let this Fowl stand as though it did go to drink at the Glass of Harts-horn Jelly, and then they will know who see it, that those two liquid Glasses serve for resemblance of several Waters in the Rock. Then make good store of Oyster shells and Cockle shells of Sugar Plate, let some be pure white as though the Sea water had washed them, some brown on the out side, and some green, some as it were dirty, and others worn away in some Places, some of them broke, and some whole, to set them here and there about the Rock, some edgling, and some flat, some the hollow tide upwards and some the other, then stick the Moss, some upon the shells and some upon the stones, and also little branches of Candied fruits, as Barberries, Plums, and the like, then when all is done, sprinkle it over with Rosewater, with a Grain or two of Musk or Ambergreece in it; your Glass must be made with a reasonable proportion of bigness to hold the Wine, and from that, in the middle of it, there must be a Conveyance to fall into a Glass below it , which must have Spouts for the Wine to play upward or downward, then from thence in another Glass below, with Spouts also, and from thence it hath a Conveyance into a Glass below that, somewhat in form like a Sillibub Pot, where the Wine may be drunk out at the Spout; you may put some Eringo Roots, and being coloured, they will shew very well among the other Sweet-Meats, tie your Basket about with several sorts of small ribbons: Do not take this for a simple Fancy, for I assure you, it is the very same that I taught to a young Gentlewoman to give for a Present to a Person of Quality.[4]

TO MAKE AN EXTRAORDINARY PIE, OR A BRIDE PYE OF SEVERAL COMPOUNDS, BEING SEVERAL DISTINCT PIES ON ONE BOTTOM.
(Robert May, 1685)

Provide cock-stones and combs, or lamb-stones, and sweet-breads of veal, a little set in hot water and cut to pieces; also two or three ox-pallats blanch't and slic't, a pint of oysters, slic't dates, a handful of pine kernels a little quantity of broom buds, pickled, some fine interlarded bacon slic't; nine or ten chestnuts rosted and blanch't season them with salt, nutmeg, and some large mace, and close it up with some butter. For the caudle, beat up some butter, with three yolks of eggs, some white or claret wine, the juyce of a lemon or two; cut up the lid, and pour on the lear, shaking it well together; then lay on the meat, slic't lemon, and pickled barberries, and cover it again, let these ingredients be put in the moddle or scollops of the Pye.

Several other Pies belong to the first form, but you must be sure to make the three fashions proportionably answering one the other; you may set them on one bottom of paste, which will be more convenient; or if you set them several, you may bake the middle one full of flour, it being bak't and cold, take out the flour in the bottom, & put in live birds, or a snake, which will seem strange to the beholders, which cut up the pie at the Table. This is only for a Wedding to pass away the time.

Now for the other pies you may fill them with several ingredients, as in one you put oysters, being parboild and bearded, season them with large mace, pepper, some beaten ginger, and salt, season them lightly and fill the Pie, then lay on marrow & some good butter, close it up and bake it. Then make a lear for it with white wine, the oyster liquor, three or four oysters bruised in pieces to make it stronger, but take out the pieces, and an onion, ot[r] rub the bottom of the dish with a clove of garlick; it being boil'd, put in a piece of butter, with a lemon, sweet herbs will be good boil'd in it, bound up fast together, cut up the lid, or make a hole to let the lear in &c.

Another you may make of prawns and cockles, being seasoned as the first, but no marrow: a few pickled mushrooms, (if you have them) it being baked, beat up a piece of butter, a little vinegar, a slic't nutmeg, and the juyce of two or three oranges thick, and pour it into the Pye.

A third you may make a Bird pie; take young Birds, as larks pull'd and drawn, and a forced meat to put in the bellies made of grated bread, sweet herbs minced very small, beef-suet, or marrow minced, almonds beat with a little cream to keep them from oyling, a little parmisan (or none) or old cheese; season this meat with nutmeg, ginger, and salt, then mix them together, with cream and eggs like a pudding, stuff the larks with it, then season the larks with nutmeg, pepper and salt, and lay them in the pie, put in some butter, and scatter between them pine-kernels, yolks of eggs and sweet herbs, the herbs and eggs being minced very small; being baked make a lear with the juyce of oranges and butter beat up thick, and shaken well together.

For another of the Pies, you may boil artichocks, and take only the bottoms for the Pie, cut them into quarters or less, and season them with nutmeg. Thus with several ingredients you may fill your other Pies.

For the outmost Pies they must be Egg-Pies

Boil twenty eggs and mince them very small, being blanched, with twice the weight of them of beef-suet fine minced also; then have half a pond of dates slic't with a pound of raisins, and a pound of currans well washed and dryed, and half an ounce of cinnamon fine beaten, and a little cloves and mace fine beaten, sugar a quarter of a pound, a little salt, a quarter of a pint of rose-water, and as much verjuyce, and stir and mingle all well together, and fill the pies, and close them, and bake them, they will not be above two hours a baking, serve them all seventeen upon one dish, or plate, and ice them, or scrape sugar on them; every one of these Pies should have a tuft of paste jagged on the top.[5]

To make a Bride Cake
(Elizabeth Raffald, 1769)

Take four pounds of fine flour well dried, four pounds of fresh butter, two pounds of loaf sugar, pound and sift fine a quarter of an ounce of mace, the same of nutmegs. To every pound of flour, put eight eggs. Wash four pounds of currants, pick them well and dry them before the fire. Blanch a pound of sweet almonds (and cut them lengthway very thin), a pound of citron, one pound of candied orange, the same of candied lemon, half a pint of brandy. First work the butter with your hand to a cream, then beat in your sugar a quarter of an hour. Beat the whites of your eggs to a very strong froth, mix them with your sugar and butter, beat your yolks half an hour at least and mix them with your cake. Then put in your flour, mace and nutmeg, keep beating it well till your oven is ready, put in your brandy, and beat your currants and almonds lightly in. Tie three sheets of paper round the bottom of your hoop to keep it from running out, rub it well with butter, put in your cake, and lay your sweetmeats in three lays with cake betwixt every lay. After it is risen and coloured, cover it with paper before your oven is stopped up. It will take three hours baking.

Recipes

To make Almond Icing for the Bride Cake
(Elizabeth Raffald, 1769)

Beat the whites of three eggs to a strong froth; beat a pound of Jordan almonds very fine with rosewater. Mix your almonds with the eggs lightly together [with] a pound of common loaf sugar beat fine, and put in by degrees. When your cake is enough, take it out and lay your icing on and put it to brown.

To make Sugar Icing for the Bride Cake
(Elizabeth Raffald, 1769)

Beat two pounds of double-refined sugar with two ounces of fine starch, sift it through a gauze sieve. Then beat the whites of five eggs with a knife upon a pewter dish half an hour. Beat in your sugar a little at a time, or it will make the eggs fall and will not be so good a colour. When you have put in all your sugar beat it half an hour longer, then lay it on your almond icing and spread it with a knife. If it be put on as soon as the cake comes out of the oven, it will be hard by the time the cake is cold.[6]

Bride or Wedding Cake
(Lizzie Heritage, 1901)

Required: a pound and two ounces of dry sifted flour, a quarter of a pint of rum, or half brandy, a quarter of a pound of treacle, the same of sugar, eight eggs, three-quarters of a pound of butter, three ounces of sweet almonds, blanched and chopped, two ounces of crushed ratafias, a nutmeg, a small saltspoonful of ground cloves and allspice, mixed, two pounds of the best currants, washed and dried, half a pound of chopped sultanas, half a pound of candied citron, and seven ounces each of orange and lemon peel, and icing as below. Cost, about 5s, exclusive of icing.

The above materials weigh over seven pounds; and with the icing a cake of from twelve to thirteen pounds may be made; but the weight depends upon the thickness of the icing and the amount of decoration. The butter and sugar are to be beaten, and the eggs added, with the treacle, and again beaten; the ratafias are to be soaked in the spirit, and added next. The spice is put with the flour, and a saltspoonful of salt; the fruit and peel are added, the citron in large, and the lemon and orange in small, shreds. This second mixture is then to be very thoroughly blended with the first. The baking tin or ring should be lined with several folds of well-buttered paper, and a few folds should be put round the outside of the tin. It should be set upon a stout baking tin; and if that can be put upon a second one spread with ashes or sawdust all the better. Unless the oven is very reliable, it will be better to send the cake to a baker's oven. A steady heat is wanted all through; and if the top shows signs of getting too dark, it should be covered with paper. The cake should be dark and rich-looking. ... A cake of this sort is not intended to be light; the amount of fruit prevents that. It should be made at least a few weeks before it is used; and better still, a couple or three months. If used while quite fresh, the flavour is not nearly so good. [The almond icing] may be any thickness from half an inch to an inch. Some modern cakes are made with a second coating at the bottom, which adds to the expense as well as the excellence. [For the white icing] ... give a rough coating first, and leave in a warm place, out of the dust, until next day; then go over again, making it smooth. use a palette knife, and dip now and then in cold water. On the following day the final decoration may be given. This is done by means of an icing bag and pipes, ... The design is a matter of taste. If some small silver sweets are used, the work is simplified; and silver bands and leaves may be bought of a confectioner. Vine leaves are pretty; and if a 'thread' and small plain pipe be used, bunches of grapes may be imitated. When a more elaborate cake is wanted, a vase of flowers is sometimes hired of the confectioner, and gum paste leaves bought; the latter cannot be eaten. The majority prefer natural flowers nowadays; and if the cake be placed on a round tray or stand, covered with silver or white paper, and entwined with white flowers and fern leaves, the effect is very good. A specimen vase with more flowers may be put on top.[7]

Christening Cake
(Lizzie Heritage, 1901)

The use of almond paste is optional. The icing is generally white with a little coloured icing for the decoration – the baby's name sometimes being piped in the centre, or a motto is very general. Small silver sweets may be used for it. In the finish of these cakes, a good deal is left to taste; many resemble a bride cake, and some are garnished with coloured flowers. Good fondants of delicate colours can be used for the top of the cake.[8]

Recipes

To make syrup of saffron
(A Knaresborough Receipt Book)

Take ½lb of saffron and a quart of sack and put ym both together in a tankard and tye it down with a bladder and let it stand a month & then strain it and put to 1lb liquor 2lb of the best refin'd sugar then put liquor and sugar together into a tankard and set it in a kettle over the fire till ye sugar is melted but don't let ye sirrup boil scum it if it wants put it in a bottle tye it down with a bladder.[9]

A Caudle for the Sick and Lying-in
(Maria Rundell, 1821)

Set three quarts of water on the fire; mix smooth as much oatmeal as will thicken the whole, with a pint of cold water; when boiling put the latter in, and twenty Jamaica-peppers in fine powder; boil to a good middling thickness; then add sugar, half a pint of well-fermented table-beer, and a glass of gin. Boil all.[10]

Aid against miscarriage
(Giovanni Marinello, 15th century)

Pulverised snake skins, rabbit milk and crayfish made into a pill.[11]

To make the kissinge comfits otherwise called ye muskadine
(Benjamin Hayes, 1649)

Take half a pound of refined sugar being beaten and searced, putt into it 2 graines of muske, one graine of sivett, and 2 of ambergrice, a thimble full of ye powder of white orris beate all these to paste with gumdragon [tragacanth] steeped in Rosewater then rowle it as thin as you can and cut it out like little lozinges with a fine rowill spoone the sett them a storinge in some warm place and so box it and keepe it.[12]

To make paste of violetts, Cowslipps, Borage, Buglosse, Rosemary flowers
(Benjamin Hayes, 1649)

Take any of ye foresaid flowers, and picke ye bestof ye flowers, and stampe them in a stone mortar, then take double refin'd sugar, and boyle it to a candy height with as much rose water as will melt it When your to that height putt in your foresaid flowers & so lett it boyle alwayes stirringe of it till you see it grow thick, then cast it in lumps upon a pye plate, & when it is cold you may boxe it and keepe it all ye yeare.[13]

To make sugar plate of all kind of flowers both in colour and in taste
(Benjamin Hayes, 1649)

Take some of these lumps of your foresaid paste flowers and beat to a fyne powder. Then sift it thoro a piece of fyne lawn and beate it up to parfet paste, then rowle it thin and print it with your moulds then store it in some warme place and when it is thorough drye you may box it and keepe it.

A Plumb cake
(c. 1778; Knaresborough District)

Take 6lb flower 7lb currants 2lb sugar 1qt cream 3½lb butter
Melt ye butter in ye cream 20 egg yolks 8 egg whites with 1qt yest. The other ingredients are left to ye makers discretion.[14]

Cake made for Peggy Lovet's Christening, May 15th, 1744
(Florence White, 1932)

Flour 4lb; powdered sugar 1½lb; cinnamon ½oz; nutmeg ½oz; eggs, 13, leaving out 6 whites; milk 1½ pints; yeast 1½ pints; brandy ½ pint; ale ½ pint; butter 2lb; currants 4lb; candied lemon peel 6oz; candied orange peel 6oz; candied citron peel, 6oz.[15]

Naple Bisquets; given me at Schoole
(Rebecca Price, 1681)

Take a pound of refined suger beat it and sift it, then take a quarter of a pounde of almons blanch and beat them very well, then strayne them with 4 or 5 spoonfulls of creame, and 2 or 3 spoonfulls of rose water; then take the suger, and 2 graynes of muske, and 4 graynes of ambergreece, and so mix it together, and put into it 3 or 4 spoonfulls of flower so beat it with a spoone, in a silver bason, then put it into long coffens [long rectangular paper cases] and bake them in the oven; and then turne them out of ye coffins, and put them in ye oven againe, in a dish to drye.[16]

Recipes

Mrs W. H. Hutchinson of Arkengarthdale: Funeral Cakes

12lb flour

10lb butter

9lb sifted sugar

3tsp baker powder

1 small tsp. carbonate of soda

a few carraway seeds

Mix all together, weigh 5oz to a cake, press out with a stamp. Makes a hundred cakes.

Funeral Bunns
(S.W. Staveley, 1816)

Take two stone of flour, one pound of butter, one pound of sugar rubbed together, three pounds of currants, ginger, seeds, cinnamon, and a little rose water, mixed up with milk. The above will make forty-eight cakes, each weighing one pound before they are baked; make them round at three-pence each, and bake them a fine brown. They will take one pint of barm.[17]

Recipes

Notes

1. Sir Hugh Platt, *Delightes for Ladies, to adorn their Persons, Tables, Closets, and Distillatories: with Beauties, Banquets, Perfumes and Waters* (1609) reprinted with introductions by G.E. Fussell and K.R. Fussell (London: Crosby Lockwood and Son Ltd, 1948) p. 28.
2. From 'The Complete Cook', in *The Queens Closet Open'd* (London 1658) fourth edition, newly corrected; John Nott, in *The Cook's and Confectioner's Dictionary* (1723) gives a recipe for making a smaller version of the cake using half quantities.
3. *A Queens Delight*, p. 73.
4. Hannah Wooley, *The Queen-like Closet* (London 1674) pp. 307–311.
5. Robert May, *The Accomplisht Cook or the Art and Mystery of Cookery* (1685) Facsimile edition with foreword, introduction and glossary supplied by Alan Davidson, Marcus Bell and Tom Jaine (Totnes: Prospect Books, 1994) pp. 234–6.
6. Elizabeth Raffald, *The Experienced English Housekeeper* (1769) reprinted with an introduction by Roy Shipperbottom (Lewes: Southover Press, 1997) pp. 134–5.
7. Lizzie Heritage, *Cassell's Universal Cookery Book* (London: Cassell and Company Ltd, 1901) pp. 1014–5.
8. Heritage (1901) p. 1019.
9. Farside family, Ms 438, Brotherton Library, University of Leeds,
10. Maria Rundell, *A New System of Domestic Cookery* (1821) pp. 292–3.
11. Giovanni Marinello, fifteenth century, quoted in Musacchio (1999).
12. Benjamin Hayes (1649) Ms recipe book: Thackray Medical Museum Resource Centre, Leeds. The book is thought to come from the Gloucester area.
13. Hayes (1649).
14. Farside family, Ms 438 Brotherton Library, University of Leeds.
15. Florence White, *Good Things in England* (London: Jonathan Cape, 1932) p. 286.
16. R. Price, *The Compleat Cook* (1681) ed. M. Masson (Routledge and Kegan Paul, 1974).
17. S.W. Staveley, *The New Whole Art of Confectionary* (Chesterfield, 1816) p 15.

BIBLIOGRAPHY

S.O. Addy, *Glossary of Words Used in the Neighbourhood of Sheffield* (English Dialect Society, 1886).
——, *Household Tales with Other Traditional Remains* (Sheffield, 1895).
D. Allen, *Irish Traditional Cooking* (London, 1995).
W. Andrews (ed.), *Curious Church Customs and Cognate Subjects* (1898) 2nd edition.
Anon., *A Closet for Ladies and Gentlewomen* (1608).
Anon., *Whimsies, or a new cast of characters* (1631).
Anon., *The Art and Mystery of Vintners and Wine Coopers* (1682).
Anon., *The Whole Duty of a Woman* (1707) 4th edition.
Anon., *The Progress of Matrimony* (1733).
Anon., *Aristotle's Masterpiece* (1775).
Anon., *Aristotle's Masterpiece* (c. 1840).
Nicholas Asheton, *Diary* (Chetham Society, 1994).
J.C. Atkinson, *Slawit in the 'Sixties* (Huddersfield, 1926).
Frank Atkinson, *Life and Tradition in Northumberland and Durham* (J.M. Dent and Sons, 1977).
John Aubrey, *The Remains of Gentilisme and Judaisme* (1687) ed. J. Britten for The Publications of the Folklore Society, IV, 1881.
E. Auerbach and C. Kingsley Adams, *Paintings and Sculpture at Hatfield House* (Constable, 1971).
Thomas Austin (ed.), *Two Fifteenth Century Cookery Books* (Early English Text Society, 1888).
M.C. Balfour, *County Folk Lore IV Northumberland* (1903) ed. N.W. Thomas.
L.M. Ballard, *Forgetting Frolic. Marriage Traditions in Ireland* (Belfast, 1998).
F. Beaumont and J. Fletcher, *The Scornful Lady* (1616).
Isabella Beeton, *Beeton's Book of Household Management* (1861) (reprinted London: Chancellor Press, 1982).
Isabella Beeton, *The Book of Household Management* (London: Ward, Lock and Co., 1901) entirely new edition.
Joseph Bell, *Treatise on Confectionery* (Newcastle, 1817).
R.W.S. Bishop, *My Moorland Patients* (John Murray, 1926).
Richard Blakeborough, *Yorkshire Wit, Character, Folklore and Custom* (Henry Frowde, 1898).
——, *Yorkshire Wit, Character, Customs and Folklore* (Saltburn-by-the-Sea: W. Rapp, 1911) 2nd edition.
John Brand, *Observations on the Popular Antiquities of Great Britain* (1849) facsimile edition (New York: Arms Press, 1970).
P. Brears, *The Kitchen Catalogue* (York: Castle Museum, 1979).
——, *Traditional Food in Yorkshire* (Edinburgh: John Donald, 1987).
——, *The Compleat Housekeeper: a household in Queen Ann Times* (Wakefield: Wakefield Historical Publications, 2000).
Peter Brown and Ivan Day, *Pleasures of the Table* (York: York Civic Trust, 1997).
William Buchan, *Domestic Medicine* (1796).
W. Carleton, *Traits and Stories of the Irish Peasantry* (Buckinghamshire, 1990) vols. 1 and 2 (first published in 23 parts, 1842–44).
J. Carr, *The Stranger in Ireland* (Shannon, 1970) (first published London, 1806).
William Carr, *The Dialect of Craven in the West Riding of the County of Yorkshire* (1828).
J. Caird, *The Complete Confectioner and Family Cook* (Leith, 1809).
R. Chambers, *The Book of Days* (1866).
Simon R. Charsley, *Interpretation and Custom: 'The Case of the Wedding Cake'* (1987) Ms, n.s. 22.
——, 'The Wedding Cake: History and Meanings', in *Folklore*, (1988) 99.
——, *Wedding Cakes and Cultural History* (Routledge, 1992).

Bibliography

H.E. Chetwynd-Stapylton, *The Stapletons of Yorkshire* (1897).
T.O. Cockayne, *Leechdoms, Wortcunning and Starcraft in Early England* (1864–1866) vol. I.
J. Collier, *Ecclesiastical History* (1840).
C.V. Collier, 'Funeral Biscuits', *Transactions of the Hunter Archeological Society* (Sheffield, 1929) III.
K. Concannon (ed.), *Inishbofin Through Time and Tide* (Inishbofin, 1993).
I. Cooper, Helmsley, or Remiscences of 100 Years Ago (York, *c.* 1887).
David Cressy, *Birth, Marriage and Death. Ritual, Religion and the Life Cycle in Tudor and Stuart England* (Oxford University Press, 1997).
T. C. Croker, *Researches in the South of Ireland* (London, 1824).
E. Cross, *The Tailor and Ansty* (Cork, 1970).
Nicholas Culpeper, *Directory for Midwives* (1651).
———, *Complete Herbal and English Physician* (Manchester, 1826) (reprinted 1981).
Currer of Kildwick and Wilson of Eshton, MS 68D/82/7/d/37 and 68d/82/26/7 (Bradford, West Yorkshire Archive Service).
C. Curtain, 'Marriage and Family' in *Ireland: A Sociological Profile* (Dublin, 1986) eds. Patrick Clancy, Sheelagh Drudy, Kathleen Lynch, Liam O' Dowd, 155–172.
K. Danaher, *In Ireland Long Ago* (Cork, 1978) (first published 1962).
Ivan Day, *Cordial Waters, in Strength and Chearfulness. The John Towse collection of English tall cordial glasses* (Chippenham: Delomosne & Son, 1997).
——— (ed.), *Eat, Drink and be Merry. the British at Table 1600–2000* (Philip Wilson, 2000).
Thomas Dekker, *Satiro-mastix. Or the Untrussing of the humorous poet. As it hath bin presented publikely, by the Right Honorable, the Lord Chamberlaine his seruants; and priuately, by the Children of Paules* (London, 1607).
Thomas Deloney, *The Pleasant History of John Winchcombe* (1626).
Charles Dickens, *Dombey and Son* (1848) reprint (Oxford: Oxford University Press, 1982).
Margaret Dods, *The Cook and Housewife's Manual* (Edinburgh, 1826).
Jean Donnison, *Midwives and Medical Men* (Heinemann, 1977).
Mary Douglas, *Implicit Meanings: Essays in Anthropology* (London: Routledge and Kegan Paul, 1975).
Drapers' Company, MS D.B.1 (1564–1602).
Audrey Eccles, *Obstetrics and Gynaecology in Tudor and Stuart England* (Kent State University Press, 1982).
F.G. Emmison, *Tudor Food and Pastimes* (Benn, 1964).
J. Fairfax-Blakeborough, *Yorkshire Days and Yorkshire Ways* (1935).
L.W. Faraday, 'Custom and Belief in the Icelandic Sagas', in *Folklore* (1906) LVIII.
Farside family, MS 438 Brotherton Library, University of Leeds.
W.T. Fernie, *Kitchen Physic* (Bristol: John Wright and Co., 1890).
———, *Herbal Simples* (Bristol: John Wright and Co., 1914).
John Field, *A View of Popish Abuses yet remaining in the English Church, for which the godly Ministers have refused to subscribe* (1572).
Valerie A. Fildes, *Breasts, Bottles and Babies: a history of infant feeding* (Edinburgh: Edinburgh University Press, 1986).
Mrs Frazer, *The Practice of Cookery, Pastry, Confectionary, Pickling, Preserving, &c* (1791).
———, *The Practice of Cookery, Pastry, Confectionary, Pickling, Preserving, &c* (Edinburgh, 1795) 2nd edition.
The Folk Lore Society, *County Folk Lore I* (1895).
Frederick J. Furnivall, *Early English Meals and Manners* (Early English Text Society, 1868) original Series 32, reprinted 1931.
———, *A Compendious Regiment or A Dyetary of Helthe* (Andrew Boorde, 1542) (Early English Text Society, 1870) e.s. 10.

Bibliography

Louis de Gaya, *Matrimonial Ceremonies Display'd: wherein are exhibited, the various customs, odd pranks, whimsical tricks and surprizing practices of near one hundred different kingdoms* (1748).

Jacques Gélis, *A History of Childbirth* (Cambridge, Basil Blackwell, Polity Press, 1991).

The Gentleman's Magazine (1798, 1802, 1822, 1880).

D. Gibson (ed.), *A Parson in the Vale of the White Horse* (Gloucester, 1982).

M. Girouard, *A Country House Companion* (Century, 1987).

P.V. Glob, *The Bog People* (Faber and Faber, 1969).

A.B. Gomme, *The Traditional Games of England, Scotland and Ireland* (1894).

Jane Grigson, *Observer Guide to British Cookery* (Michael Joseph, 1984).

Mrs Gutch, *County Folk Lore II; North Riding of Yorkshire & York & the Ainsty* (1889).

E. Gutch and M.C. Peacock, *County Folk Lore V: Lincolnshire* (1908).

A. Hadfield and J. McVeogh (eds.), *Strangers to that Land. British Perceptions of Ireland from the Reformation to the Famine* (Buckinghamshire, 1994).

Howard W. Haggard, *Devils Drugs and Doctors* (William Heinemann and Son, 1929).

Roger Haket, *A Marriage Present* (1607).

Mr Hall and Mrs S.C. Hall, *Ireland, Its Scenery and Character* (London, 1842).

W.J. Halliday and A.S. Umpleby, *A White Rose Garland* (1949).

Thomas M. Halsey (ed.), *The Diary of Samuel Sewall* (New York, 1973).

J. Hardy, *Denham Tracts II* (1631).

John Harland (ed.), *The House and Farm Accounts of the Shuttleworths of Gawthorpe* (Chetham Society, 1868).

M. Hartley and J. Ingilby, *The Yorkshire Dales* (1963).

Benjamin Hayes, MS Recipe Book, 1649: Thackray Medical Museum Resource Centre, Leeds.

W. Henderson, *Notes on the Folk Lore of the Northern Counties of England and the Borders* (1866).

Lizzie Heritage, *Cassell's Universal Cookbook* (Cassell and Company, 1901).

Robert Herrick, *Hesperides* (1648).

Raphael Holinshed, *Chronicles of England, Scotlande, and Irelande* (1586–1587).

William Hone, *The Everyday Book* (1826).

A.A. Houblon, *The Houblon Family* (Constable, 1906).

J.C. Jeaffreson, *Brides and Bridals* (1882).

Ben Jonson, *The Tale of a Tub* (1640).

William King, *Art of Cookery in imitation of Horace's Art of Poetry* (1709).

H. Kramer and J. Sprenger, *Malleus Maleficarum* (1486) (reprinted by Arrow Books, 1971).

Robert Laneham, *A letter: whearin, part of the entertainment vntoo the Queenz Maiesty, at Killingwoorth Castl, in Warwik Sheer, in this soomerz progress, 1575, iz signified: from a freend officer attendant in coourt, vntoo hiz fraend a citizen, and merchaunt of London* (1576?) Signed: R. L. Gent. Mercer, i.e. Robert Laneham.

Peter Laslett, *The World we Have Lost* (Methuen, 1965).

Claude Levi-Strauss, *L'Origine des Manières de Table, Mythologiques* (Paris: Librairie Plon, 1968) tome 3; trans. John Weightman and Doreen Weightman, *The Origin of Table Manners: Introduction to a Science of Mythology* (Jonathan Cape, 1978) 3.

Q.J. Leyden Voss and R. Heim, in *Flecheisen's Jarhrb. F. klassische Philologie* (Leipzig, 1892) supplementband 19.

Peter Linebaugh, *The London Hanged: Crime and Civil Society in the Eighteenth Century* (Allen Lane, 1991).

Longman's Magazine (April 1898).

W. M, *The Complete Cook and a Queen's Delight* (1655; reprinted London: Prospect Books, 1984).

W. M, *The Queens Closet Open'd* (1658) 4th edition.

D. McGregor (ed.), 'The Rathen Manual', in *Aberdeen Ecclesiological Society Transactions* (Aberdeen, 1905) IV, Special Issue.

Laura Mason, *Sugar Plums and Sherbet* (Totnes: Prospect Books, 1998).

Bibliography

Laura Mason and Catherine Brown, *Traditional Foods of Britain: an inventory* (Totnes: Prospect Books, 1999).

Robert May, *The Accomplisht Cook* (1660); 1685 facsimile edition with foreword, introduction and glossary supplied by Alan Davidson, Marcus Bell and Tom Jaine (Totnes: Prospect Books, 1994).

W.H. Maxwell, *Wild Sports of the West of Ireland* (Southampton, 1986) first published 1832.

G. Meriton, *In Praise of Yorkshire Ale* (1685).

Henri Misson, *Memoirs and Observations of His Travels over England* (1719) trans. John Ozell.

M. Morrissey, *Land of My Cradle Days. Recollections from a Country Childhood* (Dublin, 1991).

Thomas Mouffet, *Healths Improvement* (1633).

J.M. Musacchio, *Art and Rituals of Childbirth in Renaissance Italy* (Yale University Press, 1999).

Brenda Anne Neale, *Getting Married: An Ethnographic and Bibliographic Study* (1985) 2 vols., PhD Thesis, University of Leeds.

J. Nichols, *Progresses and Public Processions of James I* (1828).

J.H. Nolan (ed.), *Manchester City News: City Notes and Queries III* (1880).

T. O' Crohan, *The Islandman* (Oxford, 1951) (first published 1937).

T. O' Crohan, *Island Cross-Talk. Pages from a Blasket Island Diary* (Oxford, 1986) (first published 1928).

C. Ó Danahair, 'Bread in Ireland', in *Food in Perspective. Proceedings of the Third International Conference on Ethnological Food Research, Cardiff, Wales*, 1977 (Edinburgh, 1981) eds. Alexander Fenton and Trefor M. Owen, 57–67.

C. Ó Danahair, 'Some marriage customs and their regional distribution', in *Béaloideas iml* (1974–1976), 42–44, 136–175.

L. O' Donnell, *The Days of the Servant Boy* (Cork, 1997).

S. Ó Súilleabháin, *Irish Wake Amusements* (Cork, 1997) (first published 1961).

S. Ó Súilleabháin, 'Some folklore traditions of Imokilly', in *Journal of the Cork Historical and Archaeological Society* (1945) part 2, vol. L, no. 172, 71–82.

G. Oliver, 'Old Christmas customs and popular superstitions of Lincolnshire', in *Gentleman's Magazine* (1832) CII.

Iona Opie and Moira Tatum, *A Dictionary of Superstition* (Oxford University Press, 1989).

Trefor M. Owen, *Welsh Folk Customs* (Cardiff, National Museum of Wales, 1978).

Sara Paston-Williams, *The Art of Dining* (The National Trust, 1993).

Ann Peckham, *The Complete Housewife* (Leeds, 1773).

Charles Sanders Pierce, *Collected Papers* (Cambridge, Mass., 1931–58).

Edward Pinto, *Treen and other wooden bygones* (Bell and Hyman, 1969).

Sir Hugh Platt, *Delightes for Ladies, to adorn their Persons, Tables, Closets, and Distillatories: with Beauties, Banquets, Perfumes and Waters* (1609) reprinted with introductions by G.E. and K.R. Fussell (Crosby Lockwood and Son Ltd., 1948).

Pierre Pomet, *A Compleat History of Druggs* (1725).

R. Price, *The Compleat Cook* (1681) ed. M. Masson (Routledge and Kegan Paul, 1974).

B. Puckle, *Funeral Customs* (1926).

Andreas Rabagliati, *Conversations with Women* (London: Elliott Stock; Bradford: Henry Casaubon Derwent, 1912).

Elizabeth Raffald, *The Experienced English Housekeeper* (1769) reprinted with an introduction by Roy Shipperbottom (Lewes: Southover Press, 1997).

A. Raine, *Proceedings of the Commonwealth Committee for York and the Ainsty* (Yorkshire Record Series, 1953).

J. Raine, *Wills and Inventories of the Archdeaconry of Richmond* (Surtees Society, 1853).

F.R. Raines (ed.), *The Diary of Nicholas Assheton of Downham* (Manchester: Chetham Society, 1848) vol. xiv.

Carole Rawcliffe, *Medicine and Society in Later Medieval England* (Gloucester: Sutton, 1994).

BIBLIOGRAPHY

Gillian Riley, *A Feast for the Eye* (Yale University Press, 1997).
W. Rollinson, *Life and Tradition in the Lake District* (1974).
Henry Rowe, *The Happy Village* (1796).
Beryl Rowland, *Medieval Woman's Guide to Health* (Croom Helm, 1981).
H.T. Ruddock, *Vitalogy* (Chicago: Vitalogy Association, 1926).
Maria Rundell, *Domestic Cookery* (1821).
Marshall Sahlins, 'Colors and Cultures', in *Semiotica* (The Hague: Mouton, 1976) 16: 1.
William Salmon, *The New London Dispensatory* (1692).
Richard Sanders, *Physiognomie, Chiromencie, Metopscopie* (1653).
Reginald Scot, *The Discovery of Witchcraft* (1665) 3rd edition.
S.H. Scott, *A Westmorland Village* (1904).
Samuel Sewall, *The Diary of Samuel Sewall* (1682) ed. M. Halsey Thomas (New York, 1973).
William Shakespeare, *A Midsummer Night's Dream* (1594–1595).
——, *Famous History of the Life of King Henry VIII* (1612).
Caroline Anne Smedley, *Mrs Smedley's Ladies' Manual of Practical Hydropathy* (James, Blackwood and Co., 1872) 14th edition.
Eliza Smith, *The Compleat Housewife or Accomplished Gentlewoman's Companion* (1758) facsimile of the 16th edition of 1758 (King's Langley: Arlon House, 1983).
Tobias Smollet, *The Exhibition of Humphrey Clinker* (1771).
S.W. Staveley, *The New Whole Art of Confectionary* (Chesterfield, 1816).
Lawrence Stone, *The Family, Sex and Marriage in England 1500–1800* (Weidenfeld & Nicolson, 1977).
John Strype, *Stowe's Survey of London* (1791).
——, *Memorials of Matters Worthy Remark Ecclesiastical and Civil in the Reign of King Edward VI* (1822).
Keith Thomas, *Religion and the Decline of Magic* (Penguin Books, 1973).
G.S. Thompson, *Life in a Noble Household 1641–1700* (1937).
Victor Turner, *The Ritual Process* (Routledge and Kegan Paul, 1969).
Arnold Van Gennep, *Les Rites de Passage* (1909) trans. Monika B. Visedom and Gabrielle L. Caffee, *The Rites of Passage* (Routledge and Kegan Paul, 1960).
J.E. Vaux, *Church Folk Lore* (1902).
Desmond I. Vesey (trans.), '*Notes on the Threepenny Opera*', *Three German Plays* (Harmondsworth: Penguin Books, 1963).
George Weddel (ed.), *Arcana Fairfaxiana* (Newcastle upon Tyne: Mawson, Swan & Morgan, 1893).
K. Whelan (ed.), *Letters from the Irish Highlands of Connemara. By the Blake Family of Renvyle House (1823–1824)* (Clifden, 1995).
T.D. Whitaker, *History and Antiquities of the Deanery of Craven in the County of York* (1878) 3rd ed.
Florence White, *Good Things in England* (Jonathan Cape, 1932).
Lady Wilde, *Quaint Irish Customs and Superstitions* (Cork, 1988).
C. Anne Wilson, *Food and Drink in Britain from the Stone Age to Recent Times* (Constable, 1973).
—— (ed.), *Waste Not, Want Not* (Edinburgh: Edinburgh University Press, 1989).
—— (ed.), *Banquetting Stuffe* (Edinburgh: Edinburgh University Press, 1991).
—— (ed.), *Liquid Nourishment* (Edinburgh: Edinburgh University Press, 1993).
F.P. Wilson (ed.), *The Batchelar's Banquet* (Oxford: The Clarendon Press, 1929).
Barbara Winchester, *Tudor Family Portrait* (Jonathan Cape, 1955).
Reverend James Woodforde, *The Diary of a Country Parson* (1758–1802) ed. John Beresford (Oxford University Press, 1978).
Hannah Woolley, *The Queen-like Closet* (1674).
Joseph Wright (ed.), The English Dialect Dictionary (Henry Frowde, 1896–1905).
A. Wrigley, *Saddleworth Superstitions and Folk Customs* (Oldham, 1904).
G. Young, *The History of Whitby* (1817).

Index

Abdy, Rev S., 51-52
abortion, 65
Alanson, James, 92
Alcock, John, 110
Aldworth, Gloucestershire, 78
ale at funerals, 108-109
Allen, Myrtle, 133
Amersden, Oxfordshire, 109
amulets, 63, 65
Anglesey, 82
Anne Boleyn, Queen, 73
Aristotle's Masterpiece, 65, 67, 69
Arkengarthdale, Yorkshire, 103
Armagh, County, 126
arval, 91ff.
Atkinson, Margaret, 111
Aubrey, John, 45-46, 51, 56, 71-72, 77, 88-89, 90

Ballina, co. Mayo, 122
Banbury cake, 44ff.
    recipe, 143
baptism, 62ff.
Beaumont & Fletcher, 41
Beckwight, Thomas, 103
Beeton, Isabella, 77
Bell, Joseph, 50
Bell, Robert, 120, 121, 122
Bermondsey, 43
biscuits, funeral, 101, 103, 104, 105
    Irish, 133-134
Bishop, Dr, 108
Blake famile, Renvyle House, 131
bleeding, 65

Bodham, Mr, 101
Botomely, Henry, 96
Bowes, Yorkshire, 98
Bradford, Yorkshire, 88
Bramley, Messrs, 107
Brand, John, 75, 77
bread, festive, Irish, 124-125
breaking the cake, 125-126
Brears, Peter, 53, 79
Brecht, Berthold, 19
bridal procession, 38ff.
bride cake, 33ff.
    Irish, 125
    recipes, 148, 149
bride cake breaking, 56-57, 125-126
bride pie, 52-53, 63
    recipe, 146
bridegroom, 21
Bride's Cog, 54
Browne, Benjamin, 98
Buchan, William, 67, 70
buns, funeral, Irish, 133
Burton-in-Lonsdale, Yorkshire, 103
butter, pot of, 42

Caird, J., 49
Cairo, 55
cake
    burial, 35-36
    decorations, 48ff.
    plum, 48-49
    ritual or celebration, 35
    see also bride cake; christening cake; funeral cake; wedding cake

INDEX

Calais, 44
Campbell, Thomas, 137
Canterbury, Archbishop of, 81
Carleton, William, 117, 121, 126, 132, 136
Carlow, County, 133
carpobalsamum, 55
Carr, Sir John, 122
Carr, Rev William, 57
Catherine of Aragon, Queen, 73
caudle, 72
   recipe, 151
Cavan, County, 125, 128
Chamberlain, Dr, 69
Charsley, Dr Simon, 15ff., 33-34, 54
Chaucer, Geoffrey, 66
Chaworth, Lady, 44-47, 143
cheese at childbirth, 72
Chesterfield, Derbyshire, 110
Cheyne, George, 66
Chichely, Sir Robert, 111
childbirth, 62ff.
chine, stuffed, 77-78
Chipindale, Edward, 96
christening, 62ff.
christening cake, 77ff.
   recipes, 150, 152
Christian year, 12
Clifford, Lady Anne, 71
comfits, 56, 74, 76, 151
confetti, 56
Cork, County, 137, 138
Craven, Yorkshire, 57, 63
Cressy, David, 83
Croker, Thomas Crofton, 119, 120, 131
Culpeper, Thomas, 66, 69
Cumberland, 87
Currer, Elizabeth, 93ff.
Currer, Henry, 93ff.

Daffey's elixir, 70
Dalton-in-Furness, Lancashire, 109
Danaher, K., 119, 122

de Gaya, Louis, 36, 57
Dekker, Thomas, 37, 40, 41
Deloney, Thomas, 39
Denmark, 35
Dent, Yorkshire, 82
Derry, County, 125
desco da parto, 73
dessert, 13
Dickens, Charles, 69, 80
divination rituals, 51ff
Dodds, Margaret, 52
dole, funeral, 110-112
Douglas, Mary, 25, 27
Drapers' Company, 41
drink at Irish wakes and weddings, 127ff.
dumb cakes, 51
Dunquin, co. Kerry, 135

East Hendred, Oxfordshire, 88, 110
Eccles cake, 44
Edward VI, King, 73, 81
Elector Palatine, 41, 45
Elizabeth, princess, 41, 45
Elizabeth I, Queen, 38, 73, 81
Elvaston, Derbyshire, 110, 111
Exeter, Marchioness of, 81
Eyam, Derbyshire, 110

Fabyan, 111
fertility, foods in aid of, 65
Ffor to Serve a Lord, 63-64
Field, John, 41
Fothergill, George, 97
Framlingham Castle, Suffolk, 93
France, weddings, 37
Frazer, Mrs, 49, 52
funeral biscuits
   Irish, 133-134
   wrappers, 105-108
funeral buns
   Irish, 133
   recipe, 153

Index

funeral cakes, 109-110
   recipe, 153
funeral cups, 109
funeral feasts, 87ff.

Gainsborough, Lincolnshire, 111
Galway, County, 117, 118, 125
Gawthorpe, Yorkshire, 74-75
gestation, 66
Giffard, Dr, 69
Gloucestershire, 78
Goa, wedding customs, 57
Godfrey's cordial, 70
godparents, 81
Gomme, Mrs A.B., 36
gossips, 71
Grigson, Jane, 78
groaning cake, 72

Haket, Roger, 40, 41
Halifax, 108
Hall, Mr and Mrs S.C., 115, 127, 131
Hampton Court, 73
Hayes, Benjamin, 151, 152
headwashings, 79
Heaps, A. & M., 108
Helmsley, Yorkshire, 90
Henry, Prince, 73
Henry VIII, King, 73
Hereford, funeral customs, 90
Heritage, Lizzie, 149, 150
Herrick, Robert, 40, 46, 56
hippocras, 54-56
   recipe, 144
Hockering, Norfolk, 101
Hoefnagel, Joris, 43
Holbrook, M.L., 68
Holinshed, 73, 82
Holland
   childbirth customs in, 73
   musjies, 76
   wedding feasts in, 47-49

Howe, Mrs, 101
Hughes and Maudsley, Messrs, 107
humours, 63, 64
Hutchinson, Mrs W.H., 103, 153
hypocras, 144

icing for bride cake, 149
Ingatestone Hall, Essex, 47
Ireland, 115ff.
Italy, childbirth customs in, 73

Jackman, Elinor, 95
James I, King, 41, 45
Jane Seymour, Queen, 73
Jews, chidlbirth practices, 69
Johnson, Otwell, 44
Jonson, Ben, 40, 54
Jorevin, Monsieur, 91

Kaye, Richard, 72
Keld, Farmer, 99
Kelly, Mrs Marie, 133
Kenilworth, Wawickshire, 38
Kerry, County, 134
Kildale, Yorkshire, 89
Kildwick Hall, Yorkshire, 93ff.
Kilgarvin, co. Kerry, 117, 134
King, William, 100
Kirkby Malzeard, Yorkshire, 88
Kirkby Stephen, Westmorland, 109
Knaresborough Receipt Book, 69, 151

Lake District, christenings in, 82
Lambert, William, 96
Laneham, Robert, 38
Laroon, Marcellus, 51
Leeds, 28, 105, 107-108
Leicester, Earl of, 38
Lévi-Strauss, Claude, 19, 25, 26, 29, 30
Lincolnshire, 77-78, 105
Lister, John Allin, 99
Llanwenoy, Cardiganshire, 91

Index

London, 111
Louth, County, 125
lying-in, 62ff.
lyke wake, 88-89

Macclesfield, Cheshire, 109
marchpane, 48
   recipe, 143
Marinello, Giovanni, 151
marriage, see weddings,
mass, commemorative, 111
Mattishall, Norfolk, 101
Maxwell, William Hamilton, 137
May, Robert, 53, 146
Mayo, County, 122
Menning Day, 111
Midsummer Night's Dream, 71
midwives, 69-70
Mirfield, Yorkshire, 109
miscarriage, aid against, 151
Misson, Henri, 76, 100
month's mind, 111
Morpeth, Northumberland, 105
Morris, Lewis, 82
Morrissey, Martin, 118
Moufet, Thomas, 42
Mrs Eden's receipt Book, 69
Mrs Smedley's Ladies' Manual of Practical Hydropathy, 68, 70
music at weddings, 41
muskadine, 55-56, 151

Naples biscuits, 101, 103, 104, 105
   recipe, 152
Neale, Dr Brenda, 15, 28
Nelson, Mrs, 103
New York Gazette, 53
Norfolk, 82, 101
Norfolk, Duchess of, 81
Northamptonshire, 36

O'Crohan, Tomás, 135, 136

Ó Danachair, C., 125
Ó Súilleabháin, Seán, 137
Orkney Isles, 54

pancakes, 36
paste of bugloss, etc., 152
Peeters, Clara, 47
Pepys, Samuel, 76, 101
Petre, Sir William, 47
Pinto, Edward, 50
placenta, 71
plate, sugar, 152
Platt, Sir Hugh, 143
Poland, wedding customs in, 57
Pomet, Pierre, 55
Poor Robin's *Almanack*, 75
posset, wedding, 53-54
potatoes at Irish wedding feasts, 120-123
pregnancy, 62ff.
presents, christening, 81
Price, Rebecca, 103, 152
Progress of Matrimony, 51, 53

Queen's Closet Opened, 44
quinces, 63

Rabagliati, Andreas, 68
'race for the bottle', 129
Raffald, Elizabeth, 148, 149
Ramsbotham, Anne, 96
Renvyle House, Connemara, 131
Rhea, Dorothy Agar, 99
rings, wedding, 51-52, 53
ritual year, 35
Robinson, T., 108
rose-water, 41
rosemary, 40-42
Rowe, Henry, 42, 51
rum butter, 82
Rundell, Maria, 69, 151
Rutland, Countess of, 44-47, 143

Index

sack posset, 53-54
Saddleworth, Yorkshire, 79
saffron, syrup of, 151
Salerno, School of, 66
saliera, 73
Sandwich, Lord, 76-77
Savoy biscuits, 101, 103, 104, 105
Scotland
   bride-cake breaking, 57
   wedding cakes in, 28
   weddings in, 52-53
Scott, Reginald, 52
Settle, Yorkshire, 108
Sewall, Samuel, 71
Shakespeare, William, 76, 78
Sheffield, 100
shortbread, 103
Shrewsbury, 91
Shropshire, 78
shrovetide, 36
Shuttleworth family, 74-75
sin-eater, 90-91
Slaithwaite, Yorkshire, 105
Sligo, County, 125
Smith, Eliza, 70
Soar, Mrs, 111
spice bread, 109
St Bride's church, Fleet Street, 33
Stapilton, Sir Brian de, 92
Staveley, S.W., 103, 110, 153
stocking, throwing the bride's, 51
Strype, John, 73, 82
Suffolk, Duke of, 81
sugar plate, 152
sweetmeats, 74-75, 76
   recipe, 144

tansy, 65
Theydon Garnon, Essex, 112
Thomas, Sir Keith, 13
Trotula, 66
Troutbeck, Yorkshire, 98

Turner, Victor, 29
Tyrone, County, 137

Van Gennep, Arnold, 19-20, 22, 26, 28, 29
vension pasties, 44
Verlaine, Paul, 78
Vitalogists, 68, 70
voidee, 13

wakes, 87ff.
   Irish, 130ff.
Wales, 91
wassailing, 36
Waterford, County, 123
Watson, Henry, 96
wedding
   breakfast, 21, 23-26
   cake, 15ff., 33ff
      decoration, 27-28
      Irish, 124ff.
   dress, 20-22
   mass, 37
weddings, 11-13, 15ff., 33ff.
   Irish, 115ff.
   Jewish, 36
Welford, Berkshire, 51
Wendlebury, Wiltshire, 72
Wensleydale, funerals, 108
Westmorland, 109
   Countess of, 71
wetting the baby's head, 81-82
wheat, casting of, 41-42, 56
Whitby, Yorkshire, 99, 103
White, Florence, 70, 77, 78, 82, 152
Whole Duty of a Woman, 49
Wighill, Yorkshire, 92
Wilde, Lady, 136
Wilson, C. Anne, 47
Wilson, M., 107
W.M., 143, 144
Woodforde, Rev James, 49, 79, 82, 101
Woodward, Rev George, 110

Index

Woolley, Hannah, 48, 144
Wright, Joseph, 78

York, 94, 96, 100, 103
    Council of, 88

Yorkshire, 79
    childbirth customs, 72
    funeral customs, 87ff., 89
    funerals Hallam-fashion, 100